New Testament Ethics

An Introduction

Dale Goldsmith

BRETHREN PRESS
Elgin, Illinois

New Testament Ethics
An Introduction

Copyright © 1988 by Dale Goldsmith

BRETHREN PRESS, 1451 Dundee Avenue, Elgin, IL 60120

Cover design by Kathy Kline-Miller

Unless otherwise noted, scripture quotations are from the Revised Standard Version of the Bible, copyrighted 1946, 1952, 1971, 1973, 1977 by the National Council of Churches of Christ in the U.S.A., Division of Education and Ministry.

Library of Congress Cataloging-in-Publication Data

Goldsmith, Dale.
    New Testament ethics.

    1. Ethics in the Bible.   2.—Bible.   N.T.—Criticism, interpretation, etc.   I. Title.
BS2545.E8G65   1988   241   88-2863
ISBN 0-87178-605-2

ISBN 0-87178-605-2

Manufactured in the United States of America

Contents

Preface v
Introduction: What Are New Testament Ethics? . . . 1
1. James: Get It Together 13
2. Paul: When It Is Wrong To Do Right 31
3. 1 Peter: Critical Obedience 53
4. Hebrews: The True Form Of Worship 69
5. Mark: Leave Home/Go Home 89
6. Matthew: Creativity On Demand 109
7. Luke: Stewardship 129
8. John: The Simple Life 147
Conclusion: Toward A New Testament Ethic 169
Appendix I: Jesus The Teacher 177
Appendix II: Rewards and Punishments 181

for John

Preface

It is best to be candid at the beginning. The New Testament is not primarily concerned about personal or social ethics. It is not a source book for morality, nor is Jesus the one, great moral teacher. The following study will not make sense to anyone who understands the New Testament or Jesus in this light.

Rather, the New Testament is the proclamation that the first Christians made about their experience of being saved by Jesus Christ, who came as an agent from God to reconcile a fallen world to himself. Only after many years of preaching and teaching the New Testament from this perspective did I move in the direction of seeking the ethical implications of such an understanding of scripture. I have done so cautiously because of the ease with which contemporary Christianity turns the Jesus of the New Testament from a savior into little more than a teacher or example.

This book is an introductory look at the ethics of several New Testament writers. Each of these writers had a particular experience of Christ. Each also faced a different set of problems. These authors reflect diverse backgrounds, religious training, and literary skills. Is it any wonder that their approaches to ethical issues also varied? My goal has been to examine this diversity and enter into the dialogue implicit in various New Testament points of view. It should be made clear that this discussion is not so much a conclusion as it is an initial conversation.

Should there be any question regarding my approach, I take the New Testament with utmost seriousness, both in its proclamation of salvation for a sinful humanity, and for the diversity and integrity of the views which it expresses.

Readers will find it helpful to have a Bible close at hand and to study the passages under discussion. It is my prayer and hope that reading this book will be the occasion for continuing conversation with the New Testament text about Christ-centered solutions to life's problems.

It is with deep appreciation that I express gratitude to a number of colleagues who provided the opportunity to test this material. Several of the chapters were presented in more formal dress to the Southwestern and Southeastern regional meetings of the Society of Biblical Literature and the American Academy of Religion. Some material was also presented in the form of Bible studies for the Kirk Hills Presbyterian Church of Knoxville, Tennessee and the Community Church of the Brethren in Hutchinson, Kansas. Deep appreciation goes to those who supported the project in its infancy: Orlo Choguill, Dennis Benson, and Bob Green. If the book is helpful it is because of the acute criticism raised by my wife Katy who always inquired as to the pastoral usefulness of the project, both on the whole and in its parts. Opportunities afforded by the Bakers Creek (Tennessee) Presbyterian Church and the Roxbury (Kansas) United Parish of Roxbury, Kansas, the Department of Religious Studies of the University of Tennessee and McPherson College are deeply appreciated. A final thanks to Shelly Swenson who typed and retyped the manuscript.

Dale Goldsmith
McPherson, Kansas

Introduction

What Are New Testament Ethics?

We may not think about ethics often, but they become very important when we need to decide what to do, or how to behave, or what choice to make in some particularly difficult situation. Ethics—clear thinking about moral choices—are important when there are two or more alternatives from which to choose. It is at that point when Christians may want to refer to biblical passages and themes for guidance. The following study was written for those who acknowledge the authority of the Bible in their lives. For the author, this authority has to do with what could be called both sides of the gospel message. First, the Bible proclaims the message of salvation: God was in Christ, reconciling the world to himself (2 Cor. 5:17). Second, emerging from the first, is the picture of what *the believer's* life in Christ might look like as lived out on a day to day basis.

The ethics of the New Testament are the ethics of Jesus and those who were close to him—those who heard him and remembered what he said. They incorporated Jesus' ethics into their lives and into the lives of the churches they founded and nurtured. The New Testament books, of course, contain the writings of those early Christians. The reader's task in this introduction to New Testament ethics, is to listen to the individual voices of those New Testament writers as they experienced the risen Christ.

But are there not already enough books on biblical ethics? It is true that there are many books that seek to help in making our moral choices; many of these are based on the Bible and use biblical materials in developing their guidelines. However, there are no real, practical helps when it comes to spelling out exactly what *each* New Testament author believes about the ethical dilemmas faced by the Christian. It is that task which this book addresses and to which it invites the reader.

No book can take the place of the New Testament in presenting the ethical teachings of Jesus and those closest to him. But the New Testament is not primarily a book of ethical instruction. It is the gospel, the "good news," the proclamation of what God has done in Christ. In fact, there really is no one specific theme or set of ideas that could be identified as *the* New Testament ethic. The notion that in the New Testament one can find a complete and uniform presentation of the teachings of Jesus is misleading. The New Testament consists of 27 separate documents, written over a span of at least 50 years, by at least nine authors, each of whom dealt with various problems experienced by different audiences in different geographical, social, and political situations. The New Testament is thus a prism through which the original teachings of Jesus are refracted to a growing church during a long period of change. Put another way, the individual writers of the New Testament were themselves involved in the on-going task of seeking, interpreting, and passing on the original teachings of Jesus. Theirs was the task of applying the Christian message that they had received to the instruction of their own readers.

What we can expect to find in the New Testament is the understanding of the gospel on the part of a number of early Christians. As they think through and share their beliefs with their readers, we can detect their ethical teachings and moral reflections. Sometimes that moral concern is quite explicit (as in James), and other times they are concealed beneath other concerns (as in Hebrews). It is reasonable to assume that a reader might thus find a number of different presentations of "New Testament ethics." That is an exciting prospect—the coming into dialogue with a variety of persons who were close to Jesus Christ. This book attempts to put the reader in touch with the first Christian writers. The goal is to enable those early ethical views to engage in dialogue with today's Christian reader. Other books on New

Testament ethics have taken other approaches. It is helpful to survey briefly the main approaches that have been employed.

Legal Approach

In this view, the New Testament is seen primarily as a resource for the commands and specific instructions that the Christian needs in order to live according to the will of God. The major advantages of this approach are: first, it recognizes that in fact there are many specific commandments and suggestions found in the scriptures; and secondly, it deals specifically and concretely with a number of important ethical situations that tend to confront people.

But there are some problems with this approach. It is clear that there is not a specific directive or commandment for *every* one of life's difficult situations. If Christians needed to rely on the Bible for every moral answer, there would be many areas of life for which there could not be any specific answers. For instance, what does the New Testament say directly and explicitly about conscientious objection to war, the use of nuclear power, or suicide? The obvious answer: nothing that is direct and explicit.

Another problem is that it is not always clear what the "correct" interpretation of a given law should be. An obvious case would be that of the command, "You shall not kill" (Exod. 20:13; Deut. 5:17; Matt. 5:21). Interpretations of this command range from a prohibition against taking any animal life under any circumstances to interpretations which allow for particular kinds of killing (animals for food, capital punishment, war, mercy killing, abortion). Jesus' own interpretation of this command in the Sermon on the Mount equates murder with anger, insults, or ridicule directed against another person. How is one to decide among these many alternatives?

Yet a third problem with a legal approach is determining precisely what biblical passages *are* laws and commands. There are many passages which, on the surface at least, have some form and purpose other than a legal directive: prayers, hymns, confessional statements, parables, miracles, prophecies. These may or may not have legitimate ethical applications.

Thus while a legal approach to New Testament ethics has some value, it is not entirely satisfactory. It is incomplete; there are not answers for everything. It is subjective; there is no uniformity in interpreting passages. It is arbitrary; some passages are taken seriously ("You shall not kill") while others—for reasons seldom explained—are not ("Take no interest" on loaned money). This approach makes it difficult for the biblical writers to speak *their* concerns fully to us. Instead, *we*, the readers, are basically in control of the moral reflection. *We* select the verses; *we* make the interpretation; *we* apply the results. Individual biblical writers offer one or more verses which we may utilize, but *our* decisions control the activity. This approach which many hope will provide direct access to the will of God ends up too often as subjective and arbitrary.

Thematic Approach

Love. Justice. Peace. Obedience. These are the great ethical ideas that emerge from the Bible when the document is taken as a whole. An analysis of the character of God, the history of Israel, the ministry of Jesus—these will all produce major themes which those who take the thematic approach believe to be basic and fundamental principles of a Christian and biblical ethic.

There are several merits to this approach. First, it can get at the heart of the Christian message—a message that is not simply law and demand. Through the scriptural appeal to all people, the central and essential features of the Christian message can be brought to bear on ethical problems. Second, all scripture can be utilized; the limitation to legal passages can be overcome in a positive manner. Third, the results are more general and universally applicable. There is no confinement to those problems for which scripture has specific commands. Through the use of principles (such as love), answers can be generated for ethical problems which the biblical writers did not directly face.

However, the very strength of this approach—its capacity to generalize about the major ethical concerns of the New Testament in particular—can also be a weakness. There is a lack of specificity which can render any attempt at relevant ethics for unique, contemporary issues powerless. For instance, what does "love" mean in international relations, in labor disputes, or with respect to our judicial and penal systems?

Another critical weakness of this method is its arbitrary and subjective nature. It is the reader and not the Bible who must reduce the text to the theme or themes on which ethics are then based. Furthermore, when the biblical ethic is summarized, generalizations are sought and the particular or unusual is often overlooked. It is certainly valuable to emphasize the central and recurrent themes of the Bible. But is it good and responsible and biblical to omit those features which may have less than universal support among biblical writers? This approach is not adequate in and of itself to produce a "New Testament ethic." Its severest limitation is that it allows—indeed demands—that the *reader* construct the ethic out of material provided by the text. The biblical writer is only a supplier of raw material to the real maker of the ethic, namely the contemporary reader.

Exemplary Approach

This method of using the scriptures for ethical purposes is best illustrated by reference to a biblical writer who uses the same approach: James. For this New Testament writer, the Hebrew scriptures (our Old Testament) presented examples for Christians to follow. Rahab demonstrates hospitality (2:25); the prophets show suffering and patience (5:10); Job exemplifies steadfastness (5:11); Elijah is a model of faithful prayer (5:17). This is a popular way of using scripture for ethical illustration. The participants in the biblical drama are seen as models to be emulated (or avoided). This method has the advantage of being concrete and taking the biblical personalities seriously. Instead of offering commands or generalizing from principles, these quite specific stories of real people in real situations are much easier to understand.

There are some serious difficulties which limit this use of scripture. Basically and most importantly, the exemplary method assumes that the biblical story is primarily concerned about human behavior. It further assumes that the characters portrayed in the Bible are provided as moral examples to instruct its readers. Many would argue, however, that the facts are to the contrary. The human beings pictured in scripture are there to demonstrate the nature and extent of the gracious activity of God—how God loves us and rescues us from the innumerable difficulties into which we get ourselves.

Another problem with this approach is that there are just not enough examples of moral behavior in the Bible to provide an adequate basis for moral instruction in the contemporary world. Imitating the behavior of another person does not often get at the heart of a moral problem; instead, it simply inculcates behavior in a rote manner. That behavior does not really become the property of the person imitating it. Finally, it should be noted that different biblical characters react in different ways to what appear to be similar situations: Old Testament patriarchs had many wives, while New Testament readers are exhorted to monogamy (or, in the case of Paul, celibacy); in 701 B.C., Isaiah exhorted Jerusalem to stand fast against foreign attackers, but in 587 B.C., under the same general circumstances, Jeremiah counseled surrender. Once again, the use of moral examples depends on the subjectivity of the reader who selects and applies those examples.

Real Conversations with Biblical Writers

While not denying the usefulness of the legal, thematic, or exemplary approaches to scripture in developing New

Testament ethics, there is a more biblical approach. This method centers on listening carefully to each biblical writer as he shares his own experience of the gospel, and seeing how his ethics develop out of that particular situation. Let us hear the Christian story as each of them tells it; let us be involved and engaged by it; let us be drawn into it, and see what kind of behavior is called for in that unique situation. Such an approach is not only faithful to the content of the New Testament but also will be much easier for the reader to understand.

Most studies of ethics which use the New Testament start—not with the New Testament—but with problems experienced by today's reader. What does the New Testament say about abortion? nuclear war? capital punishment? This book is based on the conviction that Christians need to let the New Testament set the agenda for moral reflection by the church and individuals. Otherwise we simply are not letting the scriptures speak and we are not allowing ourselves to hear and be addressed by them.

It is the assumption of this book that the New Testament writers can be helpful in contemporary moral dilemmas; this is especially the case when we can discover that they had experiences or difficulties similar to our own. Further, the New Testament writers may well have had problems that modern readers do not recognize as their own. Thus listening with care will sensitize us to difficulties in our own lives to which we have not yet paid enough attention. For example, citizens of the United States live in a nation where Christianity is the dominant religion, yet most New Testament writers view governmental authority from the perspective of a persecuted minority.

This view of New Testament ethics can speak to the present situation in two ways: it can help evaluate and deal with the problems we perceive, and it can open us to problems we do not (yet) recognize. Consider, for example, the issue of slavery. Many nineteenth century Christians became convinced that the will of God condemned slavery. Even though slavery was accepted in the New Testament era by Christians, there were affirmations in the gospels and letters which were basically subversive to the ideas on which American society had based and accepted that "peculiar institution."

There are also ethical concerns raised in the New Testament which may no longer be concerns today, but which may still have applicability. For instance, Paul dealt with the problem of whether a Christian could eat meat that had been sacrificed to pagan idols (1 Cor. 8:10–13; 10:14–11:1). That specific problem does not confront many modern Christians, but there may well be some analogies between our situation and that of the Corinthian Christians. Is there something we feel free to do, but which offends others? The passages on eating meat offered to idols are useful in prompting modern readers to give an ethical cross-examination to many unexamined attitudes.

Most of us would not want to continue in a relationship with another person if the relationship consisted solely in that person telling us about themselves. Healthy relationships depend on sharing. Similarly, we need a relationship in which the biblical writers are full partners—to the point of criticizing us and at times dominating the "discussions" by talking about things that are problems for them but may not seem as relevant for us. As long as we see in the scriptural "advice" only a reflection or echo of our own ideas, we are not really letting the biblical writers speak. How do we insure that we are truly being addressed by them? How do we foster a truly biblical community in which voices from the past and voices from the present are heard and answered by one another?

There is no foolproof method, but this book offers one necessary suggestion. Each New Testament writer needs to be heard as an individual, not just as a contributor to a total or "average" or "summary" presentation of Christian ethics. Each contributor to the scriptures made a unique contribution. It is one of the great assurances of the Christian faith that God takes each of us seriously in our particularity. God showed that concern in addressing the divine message through unique individuals and in allowing the peculiarities of each to refract the gospel truths. It is the purpose of this book to enable the reader to see more clearly the unique ethical concerns of each of several different New Testament writers. Only by hearing the New Testament writers one by one do we truly hear them. We cannot hear them all at once just as we cannot distinguish individual voices in a chorus. In listening carefully to New Testament authors express their own unique Christian commitment and the ethical vision that flows from it, our ethical reflection may be challenged by their conception of what is important. In listening carefully to one early Christian at a time, we will also begin to acquire the building blocks of what eventually might become our own "New Testament ethic"—a topic discussed in the concluding chapter.

Why Do It? (Not: How To Do It)

Of particular interest in this study is the reason (or reasons) given by each author as the basis for behaving in accord with the ethics they propound. This might be called the "motive" for their ethics. There are persons who sincerely believe that the New Testament offers only one or two reasons for ethical behavior: to earn salvation and/or to avoid judgment. This view is much too simple and in the end incorrect. Each biblical writer has his own set of reasons to justify a certain kind of behavior. It is much easier to convince someone to do something if they understand how and why it is the right thing to do. The way to convince someone that a particular behavior is "reasonable" is to provide the reasons. When that general idea is applied to the New Testament writers, we may discover what those reasons are and how those reasons convert into ethical commands. Once this is understood, the New Testament becomes more exciting and useful as basic Christian beliefs are converted into ethical realities for our own lives.

A book on the ethics of the New Testament writers might appear to fall into the category of works—that is, a "how to do it" manual. Is there a danger that faith will be ignored? Not at all. Paul was horrified at the thought that the new life in Christ might be limited solely to belief and not expressed in action (Rom. 6: 1–4). Faith and action are not distinct entities which can exist separately. They are two aspects of one reality: one lives out the nature of being whole in Christ. When Jesus, for instance, made the lame man whole, what did the man do? He walked. He lived out his new reality. When faith is described in the following chapters, we will be looking primarily at the view each writer has of Jesus. Who is Jesus and what has he done for me? That is the vision in which each writer lives and from which are developed ethical commands.

The Plan for This Book

The discussion begins with a selection of New Testament letters written by four different authors to various groups of Christians in the first century. While space limitations allow close examination of only one aspect of Paul's writings (on conscience), the letters of James, 1 Peter, and Hebrews will be studied in their entirety. Attention will then be directed to a unique literary creation of the early Christians—the gospel. The gospel narrative is the story of Jesus's life through which the evangelist's vision of the Christian life is presented. A concluding chapter will offer a summary of those elements found in common to all the writers surveyed, and a discussion of the significant differences that remain.

Each chapter begins with an anecdotal glimpse at a modern problem facing Christians that introduces a central theme of a particular New Testament author. A general summary of "what was going on" in the religious understanding of that New Testament author is followed by a close examination of several passages of scripture. These passages were selected because of the ethical concerns for the first century Christian that they illustrate. The chapter concludes by describing ways in which the writer under discussion dealt with ethical issues and suggests how contemporary readers might engage in fruitful ethical dialogue with the particular letter or gospel.

A final suggestion to the reader might be helpful. *Before* reading any of the material in this book, first study the biblical document under discussion. This should be done for the purpose of answering the question: what is the author's point of view or outlook on life? What difference does Jesus Christ make for this writer? What is the nature of the new life envisioned for the intended readers? A quick reading or rereading of the text with these questions in mind will provide a general impression of the author's approach. A second type of question should also be in the background. What kind of lifestyle, or behavior, or character does the author wish the readers to adopt?

The primary advantage of the approach taken here— reviewing the biblical material before reading the material in the corresponding chapters—is that the reader will have a complete and direct encounter with the biblical author without the imposition of my views. Perhaps such a reading can also take place without (or with lessened) interference from previously formed special interests and questions. Once the reader has captured some initial impressions from reading the New Testament and then turns to the pages of this book, it will be possible to discuss and listen to issues that the book raises. Will you and I agree on the ethical point of view that the biblical author develops? Perhaps you have a more insightful analysis of the biblical writer than this book offers. Would you have selected the same passages from the New Testament documents to illustrate an author's point of view? By trying to develop a complete and integrated interpretation of each New Testament writer's ethical outlook, we will have to study and evaluate these writers in a personal and thorough way. Such disciplined study and dialogue can only enhance our Christian understanding and moral growth.

Suggestions for Further Study:

Robert S. Daly, editor, *Christian Biblical Ethics*, New York: Paulist Press, 1984. A difficult introduction to New Testament ethics by a team of Roman Catholic scholars, illustrated with several extensive studies on individual passages. Particularly good in emphasizing that the Christian acts out of a personal faith understanding.

Thomas W. Ogletree, *The Use of the Bible in Christian Ethics*, Philadelphia: Fortress Press, 1983. Philosophically oriented effort to show how the Bible lends itself to moral use in today's world. Excellent introduction.

Pheme Perkins, *Love Commands in the New Testament*, New York: Paulist Press, 1982. A brief study of one theme which takes seriously both the cultural setting of the New Testament and the individual emphases of the gospel writers. Good for study groups.

Fernando F. Segovia, ed. *Discipleship in the New Testament*, Philadelphia: Fortress Press, 1985. A collection of nine stimulating articles, each of which focuses on a different New Testament writer's presentation of discipleship.

William C. Spohn, *What Are They Saying About Scripture and Ethics?*, New York: Paulist Press, 1984. Clear analyses of six different ways in which scholars understand the role of the Bible in the formation of ethics.

Allen Verhey, *The Great Reversal: Ethics and the New Testament*, Grand Rapids, Michigan: Eerdmans, 1984. An excellent and comprehensive survey of New Testament ethics as well as the author's studied reflections on his own method.

1

James: Get It Together

Nobody Pushes Me Around!

During a church women's Bible study on some now forgotten topic, one of the women remarked that if anyone struck her she would kill them. I commented that such behavior did not seem to be in line with the Judaeo-Christian prohibition against murder. She immediately backed down to a less extreme, although aggressive position of the Old Testament law of "retaliation in kind." Gently I pressed further, examining both the teaching and the example of Jesus, who (while he may have shown some violence in the defense of others) always gave in when it came to "standing up for himself."

This woman certainly knew the facts of Jesus' position but seemed stunned at the thought of applying them to herself. Her pause was quite brief, however, and her recovery was firm: "I'll defend myself," she answered, adding, "it may not be Christian, but that's the way I am." Nor did she seem to think that anyone else in the room would fault her for protecting herself. After all, if she did not, who would? Looking back, I was the only one dumfounded in the room. These women considered themselves Christians, the backbone of the local church. Yet in the most casual manner, they could omit one of the most central features of Christian teaching from their lives without feeling a twinge of moral dishonesty. Here was a blatant failure to see how various aspects of life are tied together in obedience to Christ. A lack of integrity was insulated by a smug feeling of being a Christian.

The issue here is not so much whether we "stand up for ourselves" or let others "push us around." Rather it is a question of total commitment to the Christian life. Has faith transformed our entire being so that all actions are Christian actions? Or—as in the case of the woman who wanted to defend herself—does our conscience not bother us very much when our actions or thoughts are not in keeping with clear New Testament examples? The letter of James is a good starting point for ethical discussion since it is concerned with living a total and integrated Christian life.

The Religion of James

James appears to be a letter, as the introduction (1:1) indicates, but it is apparently not written to a specific recipient. James, in fact, is quite general concerning the intended reader. While there is little hope of reconstructing the specific situation of those to whom the letter was sent, modern readers may nevertheless gather insight into the concerns that motivated this particular compiler of early Christian ethical teaching.

There is an enormous amount of ethical instruction packed into James. Topics are brought up and dropped only to be addressed again later. The author has accumulated and transmitted a varied collection of the church's wisdom on the moral life of the Christian. This material is taken from a variety of sources and has been integrated by James into the Christian life as he knows and advocates it. His major sources are these:

Greek: There are Greek or Hellenistic features in James. This is seen in the form of the letter, for instance. Instead of a personal letter, it is a general one meant for anyone who would read it. It was intended primarily to convey a collection of ethical instruction. Other Greek features are found in the many metaphors which are used to emphasize, illustrate, or prove a point, (3:3-7, for example).

Jewish: James has often been considered a Jewish writing that later was edited and revised by a Christian for Christian readers. The Jewish character is clearly evident in the seriousness with which James takes the Old Testament law, and many of the examples used are taken from the Hebrew scriptures.

Christian: Some teachings of Jesus also appear in James. A few examples are listed below in parallel with what appears to be the same teaching as found in the gospel of Matthew:

Matthew

7:7—Ask and it will be given you . . .

6:19—Do not lay up for yourselves treasures on earth where moth and rust consume . . . but lay up for yourselves treasures in heaven, where neither moth nor rust consumes and where thieves do not break in and steal.

5:34—Do not swear at all, either by heaven . . . or by earth . . . Let what you say be simply "Yes" or "No" . . .

James

1:5—If any of you lacks wisdom let him ask God, who gives to all men generously

5:2-3—Your riches have rotted and your garments are motheaten. Your gold and silver have rusted . . . You have laid up treasure for the last days.

5:12—Do not swear, either by heaven or by earth or with any other oath, but let your yes be yes and your no be no . . .

It is not surprising that James should use the words of Jesus. The church passed on most of Jesus' teachings in gospel form. Jesus formed a community of disciples who witnessed the events of his teaching ministry and heard his ethical teachings in the process. The few teachings of Jesus that James includes in this letter are found without any hint of the events of Jesus' life or ministry. The result is a Jesus who functioned mainly as a teacher and judge (cf. 4:12).

Before proceeding to point out the ethical concerns of James, it is helpful to understand *why* James expects his readers to respond positively to his ethical exhortations. He devotes virtually no space in the letter to setting down the basics of the Christian faith. Faith is mentioned, but never spelled out, so there is no direct information about what the Christian must or should believe. Clearly, James does not make explicit the beliefs that form the bases for Christian action. Still, there seem to be at least four different arguments that James makes in order to influence commitment to the desired ethical action:

The first of these is *integrity*, which, indeed, serves as the overall theme for this chapter. Faith encompasses an entire group of ideas and actions. There is a unified group of related ideas, virtues, and activities which ought to characterize anyone who believes. It is like a puzzle. All the pieces must be fitted properly into place to complete the puzzle. When it is complete, there is integrity—all the pieces fit neatly into the one whole. So it is with the Christian life: there must be a smooth integrity of all the parts. Each personality trait and each action must be consistent with the rest and must fit smoothly together. When this does not happen, James calls it duplicity or double-mindedness (1:8; 4:8). He is disgusted with hypocrisy (though he never uses that Greek word) and wants his readers to take a stand against such lack of integrity by bringing all of their actions into one Christian whole.

A second argument is from *scripture*. Like many of us, James assumes the authority of scripture for guidance on moral questions. The scriptures to which he refers, of course, are the Old Testament. James does this in two ways. First, he generally approves of the Jewish law (1:25; 2:8, 12) and argues that it must be taken seriously and adhered to in full (2:10). Second, the scriptures provide models or examples for believers to follow. Christians should be faithful (as was Abraham: 2:23), hospitable (Rahab: 2:25), steadfast (Job: 5:11), patient (the prophets: 5:10) and prayerful (Elijah: 5:17). These actions are not optional but, rather, they are to be a regular part of the Christian's behavior.

The fact that James is impressed by the authority of the Old Testament in terms of law and example does not keep him from employing ethical criteria from other sources. The use of ethical material from the Jewish and Greek worlds around him provide insight and challenge. They give insight in that Christians need to amplify and make relevant their morality. This is challenging because it encourages Christians to look to extra-biblical sources for facts to update ethics and make them more relevant to contemporary situations. In fact, this is done all the time, but there are drawbacks: such borrowing is neither recognized nor acknowledged, and the conveyors of this material pretend that they are simply reproducing a New Testament ethic. A close example is that, all too frequently, some Christians identify American culture with biblical values. The result is that ethical decisions are not made with the care that needs to be given when new elements are baptized into the Christian ethic.

A third influence in James are the *special poor*. God has chosen the poor (2:5; 4:6). James's sympathies are clearly with the poor and against the rich (1:11b; 2:6-7). If what we have said about the general character of the letter is true, then James's conception of the church is that it is primarily composed of society's lower or poorer elements—with an occasional rich visitor or member. The clear implication is that God's graciousness and love have been shown to the poor in the past (according to the scriptures), and that the character of God is to behave graciously toward those in such a social class. The idea here is that the poor are deserving because they are humiliated and tested by the world. There is a difference in James from the view of the poor found elsewhere in the New Testament. In other passages their need, rather than their merit, is emphasized. In any case, there is a special relationship between God and the poor and James wants to point that out. The relationship entails certain obligations on the part of Christians. They are obliged to respond.

Finally, there is the theme of *judgment*. Perhaps more than any other New Testament book, James makes use of the threat of punishment. Judgment is presented as a motive to encourage certain behavior. The reader is told that Jesus will appear (5:7) as the judge (5:9; and possibly 4:11). So while there is a notion of "threat" in James, it should not be given greater weight or importance than the writer gives it. The threat of judgment is only one among several motivations for living the Christian life.

The Problem of Integrity

What makes Christian ethics the subject of argument and debate is conflict between desirable courses of behavior. Should one do this, or that? If there were no conflict, there would be no need to seek guidance or to argue the merits of various courses of behavior. Thus tension, conflict, and disputation characterize modern ethical thought. It was much the same in the New Testament era.

James addressed a situation that must have been common in the early church: discrimination. It was discrimination based not so much on race as it was on social standing. There were Christians who treated some people better than they treated others. James was aware of situations in which rich and important people were much better treated than poor people were. Treating people who are more important, popular, attractive, rich, or intelligent, and the like, as better, giving them preference over others—this is the heart of the matter. For James the issue is integrity. It was a problem for James and it is a problem for Christians today. There was a failure to behave in a Christian manner at all times and toward all people. Thus James addresses this letter to all Christians in general and gives a full repertoire of ethical duties, exhorting his readers to fulfill them all, at all times.

An examination of several passages from James will suggest how he encouraged integrity and discouraged doublemindedness. The first might be titled: "Don't Just Sit There, Do Something Good!"

James 1:22-29

Be doers of the word, and not hearers only, deceiving yourselves. For if anyone is a hearer of the word and not a doer, he is like a man who observes his natural face in a mirror; for he observes himself and goes away and at once forgets what he was like. But he who looks into the perfect law, the law of liberty, and perseveres, being no hearer that forgets but a doer that acts, he shall be blessed in his doing. If anyone thinks he is religious, and does not bridle his tongue but deceives his heart, this man's religion is vain. Religion that is pure and undefiled before God and the father is this: to visit orphans and widows in their affliction, and to keep oneself unstained from the world.

Even in this brief passage, notice how many ethical topics James introduces: being active (especially in obeying the law); bridling the tongue; visiting orphans and widows; remaining unstained by the world. The main encouragement given in this passage is to move and to act; do not just sit complacently, enjoying the "word" and being a Christian in name only.

Apparently one who only hears the word (the preached message of the Christian faith) is in the dangerous position of being deceived. He or she may think that salvation comes by merely hearing the saving word. Such a person hears what he wants, then thinks of himself what he wants to think. Hearing God's word is inadequate by itself. Hearing without acting is worth about as much as thinking your mirror image can be summoned up without use of a mirror (23b–24). The preached word does not stick with the inactive Christian any more than a mirror image remains after the object is gone. Or, as James says elsewhere, that person is "double-minded" (1:8; 4:8). Another way to describe the ideal for which James aims is personal honesty—the Christian person must "get it together." There must be a smooth connection between what one thinks and what one does. If there is not, something is wrong. More likely, the person is thinking thoughts that produce the wrong behavior; those thoughts are not the church's "word." Hearing only is halfhearted, halfway at best; anyone satisfied with that is deceived.

In verse 26, James begins to point out the kinds of behaviors that are consistent with the Christian life. There is the "bridling" of the tongue. Control of self eliminates self-deception. For a person who does not exercise such control, religion is of no value. The next admonition is the care of the helpless. Widows and orphans were without protection and support in ancient times. This raises another theme James pursues; namely, loving attention to all including those lowest in society. The problem of Christians paying more attention to the rich than to the poor was rampant (2:2–4). This violated the equal treatment principle that James proposed. Such behavior also contradicted the notion that God especially loved the poor.

The final admonition (v. 27) is to keep unstained from "the world." While this might appear quite Jewish and too "religious," note that James never speaks of strictly religious laws or rituals. He is not concerned with ritual purity or purely formal, external displays of religion. "The world" is that which is opposed to God (4:4). In ethical terms, "the world" is characterized by inaction (v. 22) and by ignorance of the law and the plight of the needy. "The world" denies the wholeness of life called for in the Christian life. This passage calls for a wholesale reorientation from inaction to action, from self-centeredness to Christian law, from the carelessness of the world to the care of orphans and widows. The first great lesson of James is the call to concrete action which brings a wholeness to the life of the Christian in standing out from "the world" and standing *for* the humble of this earth.

Here is another well-known passage that focuses on the integrity theme:

James 2:8–13

> *If you really fulfill the royal law, according to scripture, "You shall love your neighbor as yourself," you do well. But if you show partiality, you commit sin, and are convicted by the law as transgressors. For whoever keeps the whole law but fails in one point has become guilty of all of it.*

For he who said, "Do not commit adultery," said also, "Do not kill." If you do not commit adultery but do kill, you have become a transgressor of the law. So speak and so act as those who are to be judged under the law of liberty. For judgement is without mercy to one who has shown no mercy; yet mercy triumphs over judgement.

James assumes that the Christian must obey law. What law? His comments appear to be based on the Jewish law. Indeed, virtually everything James exhorts the reader to do can be found there. However, three additional points must be made. First, since James nowhere says exactly what that law is, and since he fully expects his readers to adhere to all of his exhortations, this law must (in his mind) include or be consistent with all of the notions expressed in his letter. Secondly, that fact raises the possibility of a law somewhat different from the Old Testament. In contrast to Old Testament law, for example, James places absolutely no emphasis on ritual or cultic matters. This is a decisive change from Judaism. When James talks about being "religious" he is speaking about morality, not about strictly religious piety or cultic rituals. Finally, the words of Jesus, particularly his command to love, and his actions are strongly felt in the letter. James knew and utilized many of Jesus' sayings. Thus we have a new, "Christian law." Why also does he call the law "royal" (v. 8)? Perhaps because it is the law of God, or the law of the Kingdom of God; the law from a king; the superior law. As such, it is to be fully and impartially obeyed.

The important point of this passage is the wholeness and evenhandedness that fulfillment of the law entails. It is not just a matter of obeying one or two commands, or of applying a command here or there. It is a matter of total integrity. Each law is to be applied fully and fairly. Each law is also to apply to everyone in every situation. Anything less is failure. Such a lack of integrity places one under judgment. The law not only directs us but also serves as a judge. James seems to understand that the law advocates mercy. One who obeys the law is actually showing mercy to others and will be treated mercifully by the coming judge.

Of the two problems—uniform application of each law and fulfillment of all laws—James is clearly more interested in the first. It is on his mind that many Christians—most of whom are poor—treat others with partiality. The rich get special treatment (2:3) while the poor are dishonored (2:6). The Christians who behave in this way become judges over the law (2:4) as they determine when and how the law should be applied. An evenhanded application of the law (in this case, "love your neighbor as yourself") will result in true religion (helping widows and orphans, good treatment of the poor), with no reduction in the quality of treatment given the rich.

In short, a Christian's behavior must be consistent. Just how far James would press the matter of having to fulfill all of the laws is not clear. Perhaps the idea that mercy triumphs over judgment (2:13b) was added to say that if one follows the law with integrity of intent—wanting to follow it and thereby being merciful to all—then one will escape harsh judgment. Taken to its logical conclusion, however, the passage means that each law must be uniformly fulfilled all the time. This is a frightening prospect, especially since James has not given the reader all the particular commands of the law. Even if the law were limited to only those given in the letter, following them would be quite an undertaking.

If the Christian's final receipt of mercy or judgment is dependent upon performance of the law, what role does the traditionally important saving activity of Christ take? What about grace, mercy, forgiveness, salvation, redemption, justification? James never discusses them. The reader is left solely with James's demand for a full, active, and consistent response to the law. The Christian's response to the law must be taken seriously and not become diluted with any theoretical discussions of theology.

Consider yet a third passage that deals with integrity:

James 3:1–12

> *Let not many of you become teachers, my brethren, for you know that we who teach shall be judged with greater strictness. For we all make*

many mistakes, and if any one makes no mistakes in what he says he is a perfect man, able to bridle the whole body also. If we put bits into the mouths of horses that they may obey us, we guide their whole bodies. Look at the ships also; though they are so great and are driven by strong winds, they are guided by a very small rudder wherever the will of the pilot directs. So the tongue is a little member and boasts of great things. How great a forest is set ablaze by a small fire! And the tongue is a fire. The tongue is an unrighteous world among our members, staining the whole body, setting on fire the cycle of nature, and set on fire by hell. For every kind of beast and bird, or reptile and sea creature can be tamed and has been tamed by humankind, but no human being can tame the tongue—a restless evil, full of deadly poison. With it we bless the Lord and Father, and with it we curse men, who are made in the likeness of God. From the same mouth come blessing and cursing. My brethren, this ought not to be so. Does a spring pour forth from the same opening fresh water and brackish? Can a fig tree, my brethren, yield olives, or a grapevine figs? No more can salt water yield fresh.

The tongue and its control is the dominant concern that runs through these verses; much of the length of the passage consists of illustrations of the problem. More profoundly, there is present again the theme of integrity. The passage begins with an admonition to teachers; what is at stake is the spiritual life of the whole community. If the teacher (leader) does well, the group will do well. This is illustrated by the parable of the horse guided by a small bit and the even larger ship guided by the relatively small rudder. The failure of the teacher is not simply an individual failure; it endangers the entire group.

James, however, is more interested in discussing the integrity of the individual. It is hoped that the teacher will be perfect, and "able to bridle the whole body." These words suggest the bridling of a horse (v. 3) which illustrates how the whole may be governed (for good or for ill) by a very small part. The parable of the ship makes two aspects of this situation explicit. There may be adverse forces against which the body or ship ought to be directed, and the guidance comes from the "will of the pilot." The point is that Christians may need to face external forces, but they are not at their mercy. We are responsible for the management of our own lives.

James starts the second section (v. 5ff.) with a negative view of the tongue. This was probably a result of his personal experience with Christians who treat the rich better than they treat the poor. The tongue is a terror and out of control in most instances. This "restless evil" is not wholly bad; rather its evil is compounded by intermixing Christian phrases (perhaps prayers or benedictions) with lies and gossip. This combination of totally different kinds of things is incredible to James. Perhaps it is similar to the terribly foulmouthed person who was asked by an annoyed listener: "Do you actually talk and eat with the same mouth?" James expresses somewhat the same astonishment (v. 10). He points out that the Christian cannot really operate on two different planes any more than one botanical species can produce the fruits of another (v. 12a), or one chemical can produce the substance of another (vv. 11, 12b).

The concern for integrity is shown in James's understanding of the tongue. A modern parallel might be the use of language, or speech. There are two positive points that may be made here. One is the importance of looking at what may appear to be a minor or insignificant area of life, and showing how important it is that even this small part be dedicated to the will of God. The second is to notice how revealing such a diagnosis (the lack of integrity) can be. It shows how one item or facet of life needs to be consistent with all others. Teachers are particularly susceptible to difficulties in oral communication since they use that faculty more than most. However, everyone can benefit from this insight.

Without integrity, big problems can result from misuse of even the smallest aspect of daily living. For James, control of the physical body means control of those parts of the self that affect not only the whole person but others as well.

Impact on the Church

One might conclude that the Christian is to act ("right practice") rather than be content with belief ("right doctrine"). This idea has been important in the Anabaptist tradition. However, it is also clear that action is to adhere fully and consistently to the Christian ideal. This consistency has several aspects: each act is to be in harmony with every other act; the law must be fully and uniformly obeyed. The result will be the fair and loving treatment of all.

There is a moral seriousness about James, and he expects this seriousness to have popular appeal among his readers. Moreover, the ethic set forth seems possible to achieve. James shows no hesitancy in relying on the unique moral legacy of Judaism. He uses in a positive way terms such as "law," "works," and "religious."

Note should also be made of the freedom with which James uses his source material—the words of Jesus, Jewish law in the Old Testament, and Greek literary styles. Though he connects passages on the basis of catchwords or topics, and though it seems disorderly at times, his basic notion of integrity makes the material coherent.

The practical success of the early Christian church was dependent to a great extent on the successful application of two concerns voiced by James. First, the poor were to be accepted and treated well in the church. Second, the church was to provide a fellowship in which all persons—rich and poor, Gentile and Jew, male and female—could get along with one another and find a "home" in what had become a very large, impersonal world. The church was, in fact, tremendously successful in accomplishing these goals. As the fabric of the Roman empire began to rot away and the structures of the central government were less and less capable of meeting the needs of its citizens, the Christian church stepped in to fill the gap. The church rapidly became a place of haven and a source of meaning for *all* types of people. Of course, there were offshoots within the early Christian movement which did not particularly devote themselves to the needs of others or to the providing of sanctuary for people in the midst of a troubled world. However, those sects or versions of Christianity which did not pay attention to the individual Christian's treatment of all others did not fare well, and eventually died out.

James's concentration on the law might seem like an over-emphasis but it must be viewed in the context of the life and problems of the early church. For many Christians, the law (Old Testament, Roman, local, or any kind of law) no longer applied because they believed that the coming of Christ had liberated them from the world and all of its involvements. James was therefore doing battle against Christians whose view of the Christian life was one in which there was no longer any involvement in or responsibility toward this world or its inhabitants.

Another factor that might help the modern reader understand the early Christian disregard of the law and any obligation toward others is the fact that they looked forward to the immediate second coming of Jesus Christ. The logic of their belief was that if Christ's return was now (or even "soon"), then there was really no reason for Christians to get involved with this world. However, as time passed and Christ's second coming was delayed, the church got down to the more practical business of living in this world. One of the tasks the church set for itself was to select sacred scriptures to guide Christians until Christ's return. The first collection of sacred texts was produced by Marcion in the middle of the second century. Marcion, however, pointedly omitted the Jewish scriptures, the Old Testament. Orthodox Christians immediately responded by decisively including the Jewish scriptures and thereby insuring that the law had a definite place in the Bible. James had seen that inclusion as necessary long before the church as a whole made the decision.

Finally, what about James's insistence on control of the tongue? This is obviously important in aiding people to get along with one another. The early church had real challenges in that area since it was the Christian claim that *all* people were included in the church. In addition, the whole problem of language was of crucial importance to the success of the early church. Modern readers need to remember that the words and deeds of Jesus originally came to oral expression in the Aramaic language, a version of Hebrew. However, the gospel accounts of Jesus' life and ministry were first written down in common Greek. A major transformation had already taken place. Language was a critical element in the preservation and transmission of this material from early times to later times and from one people to another.

When the letter of James was written, another crucial test of language was in process. This was convincing a hostile Roman government and populace that the Christian religion was not a political threat to the state, and not a collection of strange and antisocial deviants. The church had to convince the world of the correctness of its beliefs and morality. It was a major task, but as the history of the church demonstrates, the tongues (and pens) of Christians were put to courageous and persuasive use. With the aid of the Holy Spirit, the Christian church lived, wrote, and "argued" its way into the position of being *the* main institution of the western world. It would keep that position from about A.D. 300 for well over the next 1000 years. An important factor in maintaining that strong position was the Christians' careful use of their tongues, and their language, in caring for others and in explaining to the world the meaning and possibilities of Christianity.

Taking Responsibility Seriously

Faith—belief in the basics—is essential to the religious life. Letting faith pervade or permeate all of life necessarily follows if one is to be truly religious. Jesus' teachings and example gave the early church directions and indications for bringing all of one's life into an orderly submission to the will of God. The Christian life is one driven by faith and committed to faith's working through all aspects of living in an integrated way. Otherwise religion falls into hypocrisy. The integrity which we see in James is that of love for all and a rigorous and evenhanded fulfillment of the law, especially expressed in loving behavior toward all. Belief must issue in action; the action must be consistent as a whole and with the beliefs that motivate it.

This kind of integrity is crucial in a day when the moral failings of government and society are all too apparent. It challenges Christians to rigorous self-analysis. Are we fooling ourselves about the thoroughness of our submission to Christ's direction in our lives? Have we closed the books on our thinking about our own religious behavior? If we have, it is likely that we have not completely and faithfully dedicated ourselves to putting faith into practice.

Persons of faith are called to full Christian integrity. This includes a checklist of things we ought to be doing if we are to be complete and mature Christians. Such a "list" must not be a simple collection of disconnected or unrelated acts. Instead, the various aspects of an integrated ethic should cling together as the facets on a diamond to form one, solid, living testimony to the new life in Christ.

Questions for Reflection

1. Write down the laws or Biblical commands which you take most seriously. Which of them do you not apply with rigorous consistency? Why not?

2. Are there laws, rules or commands that you ignore? Which ones? Why?

3. How are our specific "sins of omission" justified? (Why don't we give more to missions? Why don't we get more involved in community improvement activities?)

4. Do we fulfill the promise of Pentecost and the purpose of the gift of tongues with our language? Can we be understood by everyone? Are others edified by our speech?

Suggestions for Further Study

Martin Dibelius, *James*, Philadelphia: Fortress Press, 1976. This complete commentary pays close attention to the moral teachings of James.

Jack T. Sanders, *Ethics of the New Testament: Change and Development*, Philadelphia: Fortress Press, 1975, pp. 115-128, presents the most positive view of James's ethic found anywhere, arguing that James is the only ethical thinker in the New Testament whose teachings can stand on their own and be a useful ethical guide to anyone without the props of a religious basis.

Dan Via, "The Right Strawy Epistle Reconsidered: A Study in Biblical Ethics and Hermeneutics," *The Journal of Religion* 49 (1969) 253-267. A sympathetic treatment of James's ethics.

2

When It Is Wrong To Do Right

Here I Stand

A heated discussion was taking place during a faculty meeting of a small midwestern church-related college. The scene could have been duplicated in the meeting of just about any organization. One of the professors had written a letter-to-the-editor in the local paper and it produced loud outcries against the college from some of the townspeople. The issue was an important one and many of the faculty agreed with the position taken by the writer of the letter. The majority also recognized that the faculty member's position posed a threat to what had been good relations between the school and the local community.

The issue soon shifted from the subject of the opinion expressed in the letter to the individual's right to have and to express such an opinion publicly. The letter-writer was a forceful and independent person who stood up firmly for his beliefs. Most of his colleagues agreed begrudgingly that it was important for him to stand by his own conscience, despite the fact that his views might hurt the college. There was an "agreement to disagree." The good of the institution, the concerns of the majority of professors, and the threat to the relations between the college and the town—these were acknowledged by the faculty to be *less* important than the right of the individual to express and stand up for conscientiously held views.

How often in matters of morality do decisions truly come from our own conscience? It is as if the individual has an innate sense of right and wrong and that each of us must ultimately listen to this "inner voice" rather than to any other authority. If one accepts this idea, it follows that each person can decide what is right for him or herself—and that there may be as many "right" positions as there are individuals claiming to know what is right. Is there such a thing as a conscience that has legitimate and final authority over each of us? How is the conscience formed? Does each of us have the right and/or responsibility to affirm our own conception of what is true, good, and right? What is the ultimate criterion or guide for our actions? The problem of conscience is one of the most important issues treated by the Apostle Paul in his writings.

The Church as the Body of Christ

The Pauline correspondence is too large a body of material to cover in one brief chapter. The focus here will be on one aspect of Paul's ethical teaching, namely, the immediate source of the authority that guides the Christian life. More particularly, how did Paul understand the role of the conscience in making ethical choices?

Paul is often regarded by many Christians as the source of numerous rules and regulations—usually negative ones—which burden the church and its members. Examples that some point to for substantiation of this view are: "To the unmarried and widows I say that it is well for them to remain single" (1 Cor. 7:8) or "Wives be subject to your husbands" (Eph. 5:22).

Before we can be satisfied with this kind of popular assessment of the Apostle's writings, several factors must be considered. First, of course, is the fact that we are reading someone else's mail! Paul was writing a diagnosis and prescription for specific problems in particular churches—churches that were quite remote in virtually every practical respect from modern congregations in America. Second, we need to clarify the reason(s) why Paul would recommend actions of any particular kind. What are his bases or motivations? For instance, if a parent receives a letter from a child requesting a large sum of money, the parent would certainly be interested in the *reason* for the request. Is it needed for school tuition? medical bills? a vacation cruise? Finally, modern readers need to grasp the interrelatedness of all the instructions that Paul gives. How do they fit together? How do they relate to his central ethical concern?

At various points in his letters, Paul makes the following wishes or commands:

Prepare a guest room for me.

(Phlm. 22)

When you come, bring the cloak that I left.
(2 Tim. 4:13)

I wish those who unsettle you would mutilate themselves.

(Gal. 5:12)

Bear one another's burdens and so fulfill the law of Christ.

(Gal. 6:2)

Do all of these instructions bear the same weight? Probably not. The first is a personal request which applies only to Philemon. The last is a general summary of Paul's teaching that is also echoed in his other letters and certainly reflects the example and wishes of Jesus. There are many degrees of seriousness and importance to the "commands" of Paul. The reader needs to see a central focus or axis about which commands can be arranged in order to evaluate their significance in full accord with Paul's own understanding. Thus we must start by clearly recognizing Paul's understanding of what is "going on" in the Christian experiences.

In response to the question, "What is going on in the life of the Christian?" the answer Paul gives is that each person justified by Christ is brought into the church, the body of Christ (1 Cor. 12:13; Eph. 4:4; Rom. 12:5). Each person is brought into this body with all the peculiarities and uniqueness that he or she had while still a sinner. This diversity—

upper/lower class, male/female, Greek/Jew—is given a place in the church. The designation "body" of Christ is wholly appropriate as it suggests both the diversity of the individual members as well as the unity, integrity, agreement, and interconnection which is conferred on those individuals by God in Christ.

The fact that the Christian is now in the body of Christ becomes the basis for the new ethical life. This is quite a departure from the non- or pre-Christian life. The non-Christian attempts to make his or her own way, particularly with God. This person is in sin. Sin is a description for that self-reliance and personal performance designed to impress God and others. The non-Christian's value derives from what that individual can be and can do through his or her own efforts. Thus all efforts are directed toward self. That leaves others as only indirect objects of their concern—useful only when and if certain treatment of others can be beneficial to the self.

When believers are brought into the body of Christ, the task of creating and justifying oneself is no longer necessary. Value is conferred on these persons by the fact that they are now part of Christ. They no longer need to fashion their actions to build up their own images of themselves. They can finally take others seriously; indeed, they must take others seriously since they are now organically connected to them. Since the Christian is now a member of a community (characterized as a body) that values the participation of all members, there exists an essential and natural necessity for each to behave with the well-being of the entire group foremost in mind.

Isn't It Right To Do What is Right?

Paul's concern for a new community might lead to the conclusion that all the "commands" he sends in his letters constitute the basic framework for the life of that community. In a sense this is true. When the plan of the writer is as ambitious as that of the biblical writers—to submit the totality of the lives of their readers to the will of God—then there are plenty of situations that need to be governed. Such situations range from obeying political authorities (Rom. 13:1) to living chastely with a spouse (1 Thes. 4:4). Things go fine as long as no problems arise. However, when conflicts begin, and each party seems to have a legitimate claim to being correct, what rule takes precedence? For instance, freedom in Christ meant social freedom for Onesimus, but as far as Philemon was concerned, Onesimus belonged to him as a slave. In attempting to resolve the situation, Paul did not appeal to the "rights" of either Philemon or Onesimus. Rather, he asked Philemon to accept Onesimus as a "brother" on the basis of the personal debt (for his salvation) that Philemon "owed" Paul (Phlm. 19).

There are many such "commands" in Paul's letters. We must remember, however, that almost every letter is written to a *different* church, and that originally no one church had all the letters. Therefore, in Paul's own time and experience, there was no single church that possessed the whole of Paul's teachings. The fact that he had to write so many letters shows us that the churches that he founded forgot or needed help in applying many of the basic teachings which he had originally planted among them.

The letters need to be taken individually, and the instructions they contain must be seen in the context of the specific incident or problem with which the letter deals, and, more importantly, in the light of a general understanding of the totality of Paul's view on the nature of the Christian life. No one set of rules can provide the basic ethic for the Christian. Paul's commands might be described as his way to move *from* the general idea of the ideal body of Christ *to* a solution for the particular difficulty at hand. In Romans, he shows that Christ gives us access to God without taking the law into account (3:21). In Galatians and Ephesians, Paul illustrates how the law has been misunderstood and mis-used. He goes so far as to argue that the work of Christ violated the law so centrally that it was once and for all shown that no Christian could take the law seriously as a sav-ing aid (Gal. 3:13). In Ephesians, the work of Christ is to de-stroy the law (2:14-15)! There is no law, rule, command, reason, or custom that can be the final arbiter of human conduct. While the law might help and human social customs might assist, their use as the ultimate criteria for moral reflection is unnecessary and even dangerous.

No one, of course, can escape who one is. Thus each is unique in the body of Christ. But these differences do not matter—they are not reasons which can separate person from person. Instead, they are helpful in answering the needs of others in the body. There may be times when the best thing to do is to adopt the particular practices of other persons or groups. Thus Paul can say, "To the Jews I became as a Jew, to the Greeks as a Greek" (cf. 1 Cor. 9:20–21). This approach was adopted in order to redeem some persons for Christ. Indeed, at times he kept Jewish practices, probably because as a Jew this is what he was comfortable doing. Yet Paul certainly did not base his salvation on, or derive his ethical teaching from this behavior.

Thus far we have succeeded only in describing the basis of Pauline ethics: the Christian's inclusion by grace into the body of Christ. Once a believer accepts that fact, law is no longer the basis for God's acceptance nor is it the ultimate guide for human behavior. Instead, Christ lives in us (Gal. 2:20) and we have a new life. But what is it that now guides ethical choices? If the commands in Paul's letters are *not* the final word on Christian behavior, and if the Apostle himself recommends and adopts a whole variety of different behaviors, each derived from different sources, where does that leave the person seeking guidance? Is it up to each individual to decide what Christ wants? That would lead to chaos and disunity within the body of Christ.

Perhaps the answer is that the "law of Christ" (Gal. 6:2) is now placed within the heart of every believer. Is there not a "mini-law" or conscience that directs moral behavior? In his letters Paul speaks about the "conscience" 21 times. Several of these occurrences will be discussed later. In Romans 2:15, Paul can imagine the existence of Gentiles who act in accord with the will of God (even though they may know nothing of the Hebrew deity) and thus have no "guilty conscience." Usually it is Christians who are commended by Paul for their "clear consciences" (Rom. 13:5; 2 Cor. 6:11; 1 Tim. 1:5, 19; 3:9; 2 Tim. 1:3; and probably 2 Cor. 4:2). By "clear conscience" he means that the person has done nothing contrary to the will of God and consequently feels no guilt. Paul himself claims a "clear conscience" in Romans 9:1, 1 Corinthians 4:4, and 2 Corinthians 1:12. Persons who hurt others by lying (1 Tim. 4:2) or in general upset others (Titus 1:15) have "bad consciences."

Paul accepts the notion that conscience is an "after-the-act" analyzer of human ethical behavior. It is of *no* help in planning, formulating, or anticipating Christian moral behavior. It can only condemn after the fact. That which plans and anticipates ethical behavior is the "new life in Christ." It is Christ who replaced the external law with the internal motivation and direction necessary to truly Christian behavior. Thus, although Paul could say occasionally that his conscience did not condemn him, this was only done after the act, and as a self-justifying remark which was really of little help in directing other Christians into the kind of life that Paul was mainly interested in encouraging.

But Paul does occasionally write of the role of conscience and it is to his view of conscience as an ethical arbiter that we now turn. Interestingly, there are cases in which Paul agrees that some Christians are absolutely correct in what they think and what they would like to do, but urges them to do something else. Isn't it right to do what you know is right? As far as Paul is concerned, the answer is that there are circumstances in which it is wrong to do what you believe to be right—even when what you believe to be right *is* right.

The Ethics of Paul

1 Corinthians 8:1–13

> *Now concerning food offered to idols: we know that "all of us possess knowledge." "Knowledge" puffs up, but love builds up. If anyone imagines that he knows something, he does not yet know as he ought to know. But if one loves God, one is*

*known by him. Hence, as to the eating of food
offered to idols, we know that "an idol has no real
existence," and that "there is no god but one." For
although there may be so-called gods in heaven or
on earth—as indeed there are many "gods" and
many "lords"—yet for us there is one God, the
Father, from whom are all things and for whom
we exist, and one Lord, Jesus Christ, through
whom are all things and through whom we exist.
However, not all possess this knowledge. But
some, through being hitherto accustomed to idols,
eat food as really offered to an idol; and their conscience, being weak, is defiled. Food will not commend us to God. We are no worse off if we do not
eat, and no better off if we do. Only take care lest
this liberty of yours somehow becomes a stumbling block to the weak. For if any one sees you, a
man of knowledge, at table in an idol's temple,
might he not be encouraged, if his conscience is
weak, to eat food offered to idols? And so by your
knowledge this weak man is destroyed, the
brother for whom Christ died. Thus, sinning
against your brethren and wounding their conscience when it is weak, you sin against Christ.
Therefore, if food is a cause of my brother's falling,
I will never eat meat, lest I cause my brother to
fall.*

This passage provides an ideal example of Paul's ethical approach. First it demonstrates a specific problem; second, a clear statement of a number of possibilities for solving the problem; and third, Paul's choice of the basis on which a solution ought to be sought.

Corinth, a large city on the major trade and travel routes of the Roman world, was home to many different religions. The religious activity included animal sacrifices. Leftovers from such sacrifices would have been publicly sold and thus would have entered into the diet of Corinthians and travelers. Christians who took seriously the sacramental significance of the Lord's Supper ("This is my body") might have concluded that meat used in the sacred services of other religions might retain some demonic power over them from the god(s) of that religion.

Some Corinthian Christians believed that idols did not exist as real gods and so they felt that they could eat anything (vv. 4-6). According to Paul, they were correct: " 'We know that an idol has no real existence' " (v. 4). There was no reason to avoid such meat. No one could be compromised by a god who did not even exist. In principle, Paul agrees with this group. It is the knowledge one gains in Christ that dismisses other gods as false.

"However, not all possess this knowledge" (v. 7). There were other Christians who still thought that idols were real and that they competed with Christ. From this belief springs the fear of eating anything that might have been used in any pagan worship service. This fear or caution was unfounded, but real to those Christians. It was transformed into a conscientious objection to eating certain foods. Thus the knowledge that idols do not exist was replaced by the fear that they might. The freedom to eat anything was replaced by the law of conscience which restricted that freedom. This command of conscience governed them, and they wanted it to govern others as well (vv. 10-13). These Christians wanted to impose their law of conscience upon others—specifically upon those who had no conscientious restrictions about eating such meat.

So in Corinth there were two points of view when it came to the question of eating meat offered to idols. According to Paul, the one group incorrectly feared the power of nonexistent deities, while the other group correctly felt the freedom to eat anything—a freedom that arose from their understanding that other gods did not exist.

There are at least three possible solutions to the problem. The Christians who believed in the reality of the idols had good reason to want to avoid eating: their conscience suffered if they ate. It implied that they would consider anyone else who ate to be acting sinfully. Their solution was to abstain. A second solution is implied in the freeing knowledge possessed by Paul and other like-minded Christians: all Christians are free to eat anything. Their thought was not that it is right to eat and wrong not to, but that ultimately, food does not matter (v.8). Their solution was for all to eat (or not) as they wished. A third solution is also possible: each group should do as it wishes on the basis that each has its own convictions and that what is right for each is truly right. In effect, they could agree to disagree. When there are a number of possible solutions to a problem, a moral dilemma occurs. Some effort must be made to rank in order the possible solutions so that one of them takes precedence over all the others.

The selection of a principle should seem rather clear. Paul is not impressed with the argument of the first group, those whose consciences would bother them if they were to eat. They are wrong. He supports the other group as correct. But what of the conscience of those in the first group? Paul rejects the solution that would allow each group to act as it believed right because so doing would divide the body of Christ.

If the group who ate meat is right, why does Paul not insist on their approach in the resolution of this conflict? This is where conscience comes in. It is the conscience of the non-eaters that eventually wins the day in the ordering of these principles: their belief that it is wrong makes them vulnerable to being offended by others who might eat meat offered to idols.

Thus when the decision is made, it is conscience that rules the day. But wait! It is the ill-informed conscience of the weak Christian who is wrong, and who is limiting the freedom of the correctly informed brethren. What has happened? The basic principle here is not those considered above. Instead, it is that *moral behavior is governed by the needs of the other person(s)*. Indeed, this is the central principle in Paul's ethic. Whereas Christians ought to have knowledge (v. 1a), there is something more important: *love*. Although Christians correctly perceive that they are free to eat, the real issue is loving consideration of others—even when they are wrong! Paul introduces this topic by setting

ranking love and knowledge (vv. 2-3): love (and giving in to
the other) takes precedence over knowledge (and the
freedom to do what you *know* to be right).

In this situation, Paul must have considered it easier to
get the more mature, correctly informed Christians to give
up what they all knew to be right in order to accommodate
the sensitivities of those less mature Christians who might
be upset by a bad conscience if they were to do or see something they (falsely) believed to be wrong. It appears that the
stronger Christians are not encumbered by their consciences! They are going to do what they know to be wrong
(in this case, not eating) yet they will not be bothered by a
bad conscience because they know that they will be doing
something more important: maintaining the fellowship in
the body of Christ.

1 Corinthians 10: 23-11:1

> *"All things are lawful," but not all things are help-
> ful. "All things are lawful," but not all things build
> up. Let no one seek his own good, but the good of
> his neighbor. Eat whatever is sold in the meat
> market without raising any question on the
> ground of conscience. For "the earth is the Lord's,
> and everything in it." If one of the unbelievers
> invites you to dinner and you are disposed to go,
> eat whatever is set before you without raising any
> question on the ground of conscience. (But if
> some one says to you, "This has been offered in
> sacrifice," then out of consideration for the man
> who informed you, and for conscience's sake—I
> mean his conscience, not yours—do not eat it.)
> For why should my liberty be determined by
> another man's scruples? If I partake with thank-
> fulness, why am I denounced because of that for
> which I give thanks? So, whether you eat or drink,
> or whatever you do, do all to the glory of God. Give
> no offense to Jews or to Greeks or to the church of
> God, just as I try to please all men in everything I
> do, not seeking my own advantage, but that of*

*many, that they may be saved. (11:1) Be imitators
of me, as I am of Christ.*

For the most part, this passage contains rules, commands, and principles. It is, in some respects, a follow-up to the previous passage and its problem. Paul seems to have been dealing in Corinth with a group of Christians who thought that they were freed completely from any moral obligations whatsoever. In this they may have thought they were being faithful to Paul's conviction that justification has come to the world apart from the law (Rom. 3:21), that Christ's death put an end to the law (Eph. 2:15; Gal. 3:23–26). But the fact that the people in Corinth were in such competition with each other showed Paul that they were not living in the body of Christ. So he quotes these people back to themselves: "All things are lawful" (v. 23). Yes, but he adds his own qualifications: " . . . not all things are helpful . . . (or) . . . build up" (v. 23).

Paul then gives general principles:

Let no one seek his own good, but the good of his neighbor (v. 24).

Try to please all men (v. 33).

Do whatever you do to the glory of God (v. 31).

He also gives some specific directions for this particular problem:

Eat whatever is sold in the market (v. 25a).

Eat whatever is set before you (v. 27b).

The reason is given in v. 26: the earth is the Lord's. God made the world; therefore, it is good. If everything is good, nothing—in and of itself—is off limits. In theory, anything is allowable. However, there are others who think, believe, or fear that some things are evil. In this case, there are Christians who believe it might be evil to eat certain meat. They believe that some portion of God's creation is to be avoided. These people translate their fears into a rule: avoid eating (some) meat. They have a conscientious objection to this particular behavior. Some of these people are Christians, but some are not. A Christian in Corinth could expect to have dealings with both groups.

Paul argues that the Christian should not raise any questions about the legitimacy of his own behavior (in eating any kind of meat whatsoever); conscience should not play a role in restricting anyone's behavior (vv. 25, 27, 29). However, if another person, in this case a non-Christian, expresses concern (v. 28), *then* the Christian is not to eat. It is the "scruples" (again, the Greek word is "conscience") of the other person that control the behavior of the Christian (v. 29). No Christian is to be restricted in behavior by his or her own conscience. The purpose of the behavior suggested here is to avoid offending others—indeed, to lead them to inclusion in the body of Christ (v. 32). There are no rules, no self-made criteria, only the needs of other persons which command the Christian's love.

The Christian is thus governed by the notion that the "stronger" (the one unencumbered by a bothersome conscience!) defer to the conscience of the "weaker" person. The weaker one would be weaker in belief, that is, one who just could not believe that God made *everything* good. It must be stressed that the conscience does not automatically make anyone correct. In fact, the one with the threatened conscience is burdened with the wrong view! What conscience does is to inflict guilt and bad feelings on its owner, causing the owner to feel that the person who behaves differently is evil or sinful. This disrupts the faith community and the fellowship within the body of Christ. In this situation, conscience causes the problem! The strong Christian must give up doing what is enjoyable and perfectly permissible in order to prevent separation of the members of the body.

Verses 29–30 indicate Paul's distress at being put in a situation where he had to limit his behavior to fit the limiting expectations of other persons. One could object—on principle—that freedom in Christ should not be constricted because some ill-informed and weak-faithed brother or sister is worried about certain behaviors. However, the more important principle for Paul is not "what I want" but "what you want"; it is not "what I (even on correct principle) believe to be correct," but "what you (even when wrong) hold to be correct." Love for one another is the constant theme in Paul. It dictates that each be ready to give in to the other.

This is the basic meaning of all of Paul's admonitions to submit to one another (Eph. 5:21; Gal. 5:13; Phil. 2:4; 1 Thes. 4:9). If some do not submit themselves to other Christians, it is probably because they are still operating on the popular view of religious ethics which assumes that there is a set of rules which an individual (or community) must follow. Often these rules are more important than the sensitivities and needs of others. Paul is clearly amazed by this state of affairs (vv. 29b-30), but he does not let his convictions or his personal feelings lead him to insist on his own way.

The conclusion is that one does not need to pay heed to conscience, unless it is to the tender conscience of a weaker, ill-informed, weak-faithed brother or sister. What is right is to be considerate of other persons. If others are so "weak" that their consciences cannot tolerate certain of our behaviors, then clearly, we are not to offend them. This is not because certain behaviors are right or wrong in and of themselves, but out of consideration for their consciences.

Romans 14:1-4

> *As for the man who is weak in faith, welcome him, but not for disputes over opinions. One believes he may eat anything, while the weak man eats only vegetables. Let not him who eats despise him who abstains, and let not him who abstains pass judgement on him who eats; for God has welcomed him. Who are you to pass judgement on the servant of another? It is before his own master that he stands or falls. And he will be upheld, for the Master is able to make him stand.*

A general theme for these last chapters of Romans (12-15) could be "the importance of getting along with one another." In this passage, Paul returns to a treatment of the kinds of tensions that can exist between persons who have different ideas of what is appropriate behavior. One's private views and actions are always subject to the reaction of others. Instead of cautioning the strong Christians (who know food restrictions are unnecessary) to sacrifice their freedom for the other, he cautions both of them to do whatever they do in the light of the coming judgment and not to judge the other. There is an implicit warning against establishing what we would call a conscience, that is, views one holds and sets up as criteria which must be met in order to win approval. Paul will have none of that. It is God whom we serve. It is before God that we are judged. Our task is to get along with one another.

There is room in the body of Christ for those who have incorrect and immature ideas and behaviors. That is because Christians are joined to the body on the basis of Christ's work, not on the basis of their own good ideas or actions. The Christian is free from earning salvation, free from the law, free from sin, free from conscience—but not free from the needs of others.

Criteria and commands for mutual upbuilding abound in the next two chapters of Romans (14-15): "Let us . . . decide never to put a stumbling block or hindrance in the way of a brother (14:13)." "Let us then pursue what makes for peace and for mutual upbuilding (14:19)." "Let each of us please his neighbor for his good, to edify him (15:2)." Concern for others emerges with clarity as the basic ethical strategy for making a human reality of the body of Christ. This is supported by a number of passages elsewhere in Paul's writings:

Bear *one another's* burdens.

(Gal. 6:2a)

We . . . are . . . individually members of *one another* . . . love *one another* with brotherly affection; outdo *one another* in showing honor.

(Rom. 12:5-10)

For you were called to freedom, brethren; only do not use your freedom as an opportunity for the flesh, but through love be servants of *one another.*

(Gal. 5:13)

Be subject to *one another* out of reverence for Christ.

(Eph. 5:21)

Law was from God, yet it had a very limited function. It was given well after the gift of gracious promise to mankind (Gal. 3:17). It was given by an intermediary (Gal. 3:19) and not by God himself. It functioned only for a limited time—until Christ came (Gal. 3:24). Thus the law had a basically negative role. It was to point out what might be wrong, but it could not creatively prescribe the positive actions of love (Gal. 5:23). Law was not a help in framing an ethical system. The Christian cannot be governed by an external set of rules because no set of rules can account for all possible cases. There is also a tendency for persons who take laws seriously to pay more attention to them than to other persons.

Following Rules: The Early Rounds of a Continuing Battle

Those who became Christians directly from their Jewish background knew no personal conscience nor any term for it, but they did have the law which they studied both personally and as a religious community. Paul felt that the law—although God given—had been misused. Some used it as a barrier to separate Jews from others. For others, it was to be followed strictly in an attempt to impress God. Paul battled against allowing the law such a false place within Christianity. It was not the basis upon which God expected to base a relationship with people. It was not the basis for formulating Christian ethical life. It was not the basis for judging sin. Paul insisted relentlessly that the law was *not* God's measuring stick for offering himself to human beings. In practical terms, Paul also recognized the divisive effects of the traditional use of the law. In fact, he realized that the use of any law, custom, tradition, practice, habit, or human criterion would have disastrous effects on the preaching of the gospel and the formation of churches. Such an approach to religion would result in the exclusion of many for whom Christ had lived and died.

While the Greek world was not particularly enthusiastic about the notion of law as the Jews had traditionally cherished and practiced it, the role of the individual conscience was another matter. In popular religions and in classical philosophical systems, the devout Greek was encouraged to live according to conscience or internalized principles of reason. This popular and broadly based notion threatened to transfer the Jewish interest in obeying the law over to the obedience to a conscience. For Paul, both were sinful perversions of human life. They were self-gratifying approaches of people who wanted to secure for themselves that which only God can provide. They were both individualized, orienting the individual to a list of "do's and do not's." What was necessary was to be relieved or liberated from lists and made sensitive to other persons.

Paul wrote that Christians have been given the ministry of reconciliation (2 Cor. 5:18). His view was aimed at the wholeness of the faith community, directing Christians toward one another, rather than toward a Greek or modern view of conscience. His extended treatments of conscience are more in terms of cautions against abusing this Greek-based faculty than they are confidence in the power of conscience to be a positive ethical guide. Paul needed to prevent the law-perversion of Judaism from emerging in the gentile church under the new guise of conscience-legalism.

This proved a difficult challenge. Many early Christians, both ex-Jews and new gentile converts, were enthusiastically supportive of a strict Christian ethic that could be codified and taught to others. Paul remains a beacon of Christian freedom from any rules that could impede service to others and might enhance selfishness.

Paul's Ethic and Individual Conscience Today

Paul's ethical teaching continues to commend itself to the contemporary church. Its strengths are: first, its basis within the reality of Christian salvation; second, its simplicity; third, its universal appeal and applicability; and fourth, its humaneness.

Paul's ethical teaching *agrees* perfectly with his understanding of salvation. Just as a person is released from the bondage, isolation, and ignorance of sin by the grace of God in Christ, one is freed from selfishness and enabled to live for those others for whom Christ died and arose. Human relations become the primary area of ethics and the stage for the fullest development of each person. This ethic is consistent with Paul's understanding of the Christian's new condition, and it makes sense out of the particular suggestions (not laws or rules) found in his letters.

Paul's ethical teaching is *simple* because it dispenses with the (Jewish) law—and indeed any set of rules. One can "travel light." The brother or sister is to be loved in terms that are helpful to his or her situation. Through this simplicity of concern, the entire body of Christ will be built up.

Paul's ethical teaching is *universal* because one can live the Christian life in any social environment. Christ is above culture. No particular social custom or restriction can separate God from humanity nor humanity from itself. Christ came to cut through all such isolating restrictions, thus the disciple need not let them separate one from others.

Paul's ethical teaching is *humane* because people—real flesh and blood individuals—are the crucial center of the ethics. No time or effort is wasted on protecting oneself from a supposedly harmful and evil world. No energy need be invested in doing irrelevant "works" which in some abstract sense are "good."

The use of "conscience" in the modern western world is quite different from that of Paul. We tend to see conscience as a faculty that each person possesses. We believe it can anticipate actions and help make moral choices. It is something we carry within us, the internalization of laws or rules or principles. We use it to justify, often in advance, our actions; and we can use it to evaluate the actions of others also. The current and popular individualistic understanding of religion has led us to believe that we have a personalized, internalized faculty that guides our own behavior. Further, we have accepted the notion that each may have one's own conscience, based on or informed by whatever set of values one prefers. Finally, we have encouraged and praised the strict adherence of each to his or her own conscience as a supremely important commitment, almost without regard for the content or consequences of such a commitment. The important thing often seems to be faithfulness to our own consciences, being true to ourselves. The impact on others is not as important as our own feelings.

It seems clear Paul would have rejected these views of conscience and Christianity as utterly selfish and arrogant, and as a perverse kind of legalism. "Let your conscience be your guide," is an utterly impossible exhortation for Paul to have made. The individual conscience can do nothing before a moral question arises. It can only respond, like a backseat driver or a Monday morning quarterback. For Paul the need of the other person—premised on a common rebirth into the body of Christ—imposes specific ethical demands upon Christians. The basis for such an ethic is clearly in Christ and the new set of loving relationships that are possible through him. Christian behavior ought to be determined by the needs and sensitivities of others. Actions should not be the result of individually constructed, protective consciences that serve only personal needs.

Paul has much to teach the church today about the importance of other persons serving as the "law" to ethical behavior. He is a ruthless critic of those who feel it is important to govern behavior with codified rules rather than with the needs of the brother or sister. Dialogue with Paul will lead to questioning the "rules" that we have often taken more seriously than we have the persons for whom Christ died to redeem.

Questions for Reflection

1. What is your description or definition of what it means to be a Christian? What is "going on" in your church or Christian fellowship group? To what extent is the experience there truly the "body of Christ?" Are there actually different kinds of members? if so; describe those differences and how each contributes to the "body's" well-being.

2. What are the basic values or rules that you would never compromise—even if it meant hurting someone else's feelings? Why are those values more important to you or your group than the needs of other people.

3. Take a specific contemporary ethical problem (medical, political, environmental) and list various ways to solve it. Work through a solution following Paul's approach. How might it work? Why or why not?

4. Describe characteristics of a "strong" Christian. Is your definition the same as Paul's? In ethical disagreements among Christians, how should we decide who is the "stronger" (and what it means to be "stronger") and who is the "weaker."

Suggestions for Further Study

Robert Austgen, *Natural Motivation in the Pauline Epistles*, Notre Dame: University of Notre Dame Press, 1966; shows the full range of arguments that Paul used to encourage Christians to live the Christian life.

Robert Daly, Ed., *Christian Biblical Ethics*, New York: Paulist Press, 1984; includes several short studies of Pauline ethics using 1 Cor. 7:8–24 (marriage), Rom. 9–11 (dissent) and Rom. 13:1–7 (politics).

Victor Furnish, *Theology and Ethics in Paul*, New York: Abingdon, 1968; clearly develops the important point that Paul's ethical concerns are radically integral to his basic religious beliefs and grow out of those beliefs.

Richard Horsley, "Consciousness and Freedom among the Corinthians; 1 Corinthians 8-10," *Catholic Biblical Quarterly* 40 (1978) 574-589; points out that freedom of conscience was the problem, not the solution, in Corinth.

Richard Longenecker, *New Testament Social Ethics for Today*, Grand Rapids, Michigan: Eerdmans, 1984; an ethical interpretation of Galatians 3:28 and an analysis of *how* a New Testament ethic might be interpreted and applied today.

Thomas Ogletree, *The Use of the Bible in Christian Ethics*, Philadelphia: Fortress Press, 1983; an excellent summary of Paul's ethical outlook as one that enables the acceptance of all people because Christ has liberated Christians from dependence upon human systems.

C. A. Pierce, *Conscience in the New Testament*, Studies in Biblical Theology, #15, Chicago: Allenson, 1955; a major study of the biblical understanding of conscience; focuses primarily on the Pauline texts.

Jack Sanders, *Ethics in the New Testament: Change and Development*, Philadelphia: Fortress Press, 1975; includes a critical view of Paul's thought from a less than enthusiastic perspective.

3

1 Peter: Critical Obedience

Conflicting Demands

Three young friends reach age 18 and are faced with the obligation to register for the draft. The first has no difficulty in obeying the law of the land. For him, the law, the expectations of society, and his family traditions have prepared him to expect and anticipate this opportunity to present himself for the possible defense of his country. For him, what is legally demanded and what is morally and culturally expected are identical. He has no conflict and thus no moral problem. While he may have some other conflicts in terms of sexual morality, career choices, or whether or not to share homework answers with a fellow student, on the question of draft registration there is no moral conflict.

The second 18-year old has no problem either; he lives under the same legal system and its demands, but he does not register for the draft. Why not? Because the expectations placed upon him by his family, church, and other primary relationships are such that conscientious objection to the draft, to the military, and to war are a central part of his moral and religious life. There is clearly a conflict between this youth's legal situation and the expectations of his faith. However, for him there is no problem because he has already decided that his first allegiance is to God (whom he believes opposes war and all of its implications). Only secondarily does he owe obedience to human governments.

The third youth, however, experiences a real dilemma. He is fully aware of the legal obligations he faces. At the same time he is aware of other claims to his allegiance. Perhaps there is a friend with religiously based conscientious objection to the military and to war who influences him. Perhaps, though he belongs to a church without a particularly peace-oriented tradition, he concludes that God really does not want people to fight or even to prepare for fighting. For whatever reason, he has developed new ideas of duty and his allegiances. He now does not know exactly where to place his allegiance. Whom should he obey, his new ideas or the state? This is a moral dilemma and he needs to analyze his situation, his options, and the reasons why each option seems worth considering.

Each person lives as a member of a social, political, and cultural entity that we will designate "community." In the case of the third youth, the young man lives in a community that has come to a conclusion about establishing a draft. The community decided in a legally approved manner that there would be a universal registration of all 18-year-old males. For the most part, people usually agree to most of the decisions arrived at by their communities.

But this young man has also been challenged with a different option for his behavior. This challenge may have come to him in a very private and personal way, or it may have come as he participated in some other group, such as in a church or university setting. Either way, here is an example of conflicting demands, each supported by compelling reasons, and a decision must be made.

Conflicting claims. The readers to whom 1 Peter wrote experienced them. Christians today experience them. Young men not only have to deal with whether or not to sign up for the draft, but conflicting claims for allegiance confront Christians in virtually every area of life. In today's pluralistic society, there are enormous numbers of different ideas on just about any issue, from choice of a job to medical care to sex to social and political questions. What should Christians do? How should decisions be made? To whom do they listen? What authority do they obey? Things may even be more ethically complex in modern society than in the situation of 1 Peter. Today the conflict of demands for our allegiance may come from *within* the church itself!

The Household of Faith in Suffering Obedience

1 Peter is addressed to Christians who see themselves as clearly separated from the world. The strategy of the letter is to encourage the recipients to hold together as the true household of God while at the same time taking the world seriously.

From a quick reading of 1 Peter, it is clear that two things are happening: the intended readers have been incorporated into a new life in God, but their efforts to live within that new situation are threatened by forces exerted on them by the surrounding society. The conflict of those two realities creates the ethical dilemma which 1 Peter addresses.

Why is the church—which is not *of* the world—expected to live *in* the world rather than to move out and away from it? 1 Peter stresses three reasons: First, God indirectly authorizes civil authorities; they function for the benefit of society. Second, Jesus was fully involved with "the world." Third, life in the world is a means to evangelize the world.

The letter is addressed to Christians who should not see themselves as their pagan neighbors see them (as residents of a particular locality), but as reborn into a totally new reality that began with the resurrection of the unjustly punished Jesus. This new life is an actuality that has been created for and given to the Christian as a gift, and not as something earned. This is clear in the expressions used by the author: "We have been born anew (1:3) . . . you were ransomed (1:8) . . . you have been born anew (1:23) . . . be yourselves built into a spiritual house (1:18) . . . you are a chosen race (2:9) . . . you received mercy (2:10)." Christians have been transformed. It is the great fact of their new lives, and it is upon that fact that 1 Peter bases all ethical commands. What does it mean to be a new person? The most fundamental feature of this new reality is that of *obedient submission to the will of God* (1:2; 1:14; 2:13; 2:18; 3:1; 4:2; 5:5).

The picture of God is that of the truly just judge (3:12; 4:5; 4:17) who will give Jesus his due reward in place of the death which the worldly judges had mistakenly given him. This same God may also be awaiting Christians (4:17) and it is reasonable to assume that he will judge their obedience. What is that obedience? What behavior is it that reveals or expresses such obedience, such a new life?

Love of other Christians is the first ethical principal mentioned (1:22) and it is stressed as "above all" the most important ethical imperative (4:8; 2:17). Its focus is clearly on others. Love implies a number of additional ethical commands: hospitality (4:9), dealing kindly with social inferiors (5:3; 3:7), and being obedient to superiors (2:13–14; 2:18; 3:1; 5:5).

The Problem of Conflicting Demands

Since God is the creator and judge, it may be assumed that the world in all its parts operates according to God's will. Society as a whole and government in particular can be expected to do the will of God and to encourage others in doing it (2:13–14). However, it is sadly the case that society as a whole does not know the will of God (1:14; 1:18; 2:9) and the government at times punishes those who in fact are doing right and obeying God (2:22–23).

The conflict arises as Christians become aware of opposing demands. For instance, the "world" (secular living) encourages "vain passions"—perhaps illustrated by physical or cosmetic adornment of women (3:3). Christians are not to comply.

The government and those in authority should reward good and punish evil (2:14). It seems, however, that the recipients of this letter experienced two kinds of problems. The first is that the government demanded actions contrary to the will of God as the Christians understood that will. The second is that there were cases when Christians behaved in full accord with the law but still suffered under government and/or at the hands of an overly zealous populace.

Thus Christians come into conflict with one another because of the conflicting demands of various authorities. This is clear on a number of grounds. First, the fact that Christians were suffering persecution—some of which was unjust and undeserved—implied that the state was not living up to its task of praising right and punishing wrong (cf. 4:16-17). Second, in the lengthy section on servants, an extended discussion of Christ appears (2:21-24). Though guiltless, Jesus obediently submitted to the state without reviling or threatening anyone. The implication was that Jesus' trust was in a truly just judge (v. 23), namely God. This cannot fail to imply criticism of the government for its failure to do its proper task with regard to the guiltless Jesus.

Should the Christian obey the state? If the state judges incorrectly, should the Christian seek vengeance as the nonbeliever would likely do? Should the Christian obey God? And if punished by the state, should the Christian behave meekly as did Jesus?

In the major conflict—that between God's will and state actions—the basic decision for Christians is clear: God is to be obeyed. This is not, however, a license to rebel against the state. Rather, it is to submit to whatever punishment the government wants to inflict on a person. The criteria for evaluating the justice of a government's actions come from God.

Obedience of servants to masters is a similar derivative from the idea of obedience to God. But it is also the most appropriate place in the letter to place the discussion of the significance of Jesus who himself was obedient and whose life and death are examples of obedience for all Christians to follow.

1 Peter's lack of any commands to political leaders or masters reflects both the socio-political situations of the Asian Christians to whom the letter is addressed as well as the outlook of the author. It is an outlook in which obedient

submission is the primary form of Christian (ethical) behavior.

The Ethics of 1 Peter
1 Peter 2:11–15

> *Beloved I beseech you as aliens and exiles to ab-stain from the passions of the flesh that wage war against your soul. Maintain good conduct among the Gentiles, so that in case they speak against you as wrongdoers, they may see your good deeds and glorify God on the day of visitation. Be subject for the Lord's sake to every human institution, whether it be to the emperor as supreme, or to governors as sent by him to punish those who do wrong and to praise those who do right. For it is God's will that by doing right you should put to silence the ignorance of foolish men.*

The idea of "doing good" seems to be a peculiarly Petrine theme. "To do good" occurs in 2:15, 2:20, 3:6 and 3:17. It also occurs three times in Luke (6:9, 33, 35) and in 3 John 11. In Luke there is a clear concern to benefit others. In 3 John, it is not clear what constitutes "doing good." "Well doing" (the noun form) occurs only in 1 Peter 4:19. "Do-gooder" (noun) occurs in 1 Peter 2:14. A total of 6 of the 10 New Testament occurrences of some form of "doing good" are in 1 Peter.

What is the "good" behavior to which Christians are called (2:12)? Does Peter assume his readers already know? If so, is it specifically Christian behavior or is it a widely accepted pattern of behavior known and admired throughout the Gentile world? Exactly what behaviors are specified? Does Peter view them as specific to one particular place and time? Could Christian good works then differ from place to place and time to time? Or are they understood to be universally valid and binding so that a Christian would always have the same set of behavioral expectations everywhere, regardless of the circumstances? If this is the case, then any study of 1 Peter must seek diligently to specify those "good works" with clarity. The main responsibility of the Christian with regard to government and society is to do good works and avoid bad works. What are these works? Are they defined as good by the Christians or does the government and/or society at large define them?

An initial temptation might be to supply a list of good works taken from our own thoughts and experiences or from biblical teachings found in parts of the Bible other than 1 Peter. But this will not do. Christians may not read their own ideas into the words of Peter. Nor is there justification in assuming that Peter endorses ideas about good works found in other biblical writers.

Instead, the reader must look into the author's situation. Peter rejects the idea that society or the world sets the agenda of works for the Christian to perform. Good deeds are mentioned (2:12) in a way that implies they are not simply actions which are dictated by the morality of the gentiles. Rather, they are something that the gentiles might later—on closer inspection—come to see as good works.

The first specific behavior that 1 Peter mentions as a good deed is submissive obedience to the emperor and other agencies of government (2:13-14). Verse 15 confirms that subjection to the authorities is a good. Good works are not possible without obedience. Obedience is understood as a precondition to other good deeds.

Doing right is not simply being obedient (unless it is equated with active submission to the will of God). It is connected several times (4:19; 3:17; 2:20; 2:12) with unjust suffering inflicted upon those who do not deserve it. Good works also mean loving within the Christian community and maintaining a nonvindictive manner in the difficult relations with those outside the church (3:8-11).

The only clear suggestion of a specific behavior is that of obedience or subjection to authority. That means that each authority is supposed to know how to manage subordinates: God, state, master, husband. (Incidentally, this would explain why instructions to rulers and masters are lacking in the letter since there may not have been government officials or

slave owners in the community 1 Peter addressed.) Each
person in a subservient position is to accept the instructions
as they come to him or her from the particular authority to
whom he or she is responsible.

To learn what a good work is, one should look to the
authority to whom he or she submits. God's will is revealed
in the context of the new reality of the Christian life (1:13ff;
3:21), in the (Old Testament) scripture (1:25; 3:5-6; 3:10-
12; 5:5) and in the instruction and care in the church (3:21;
4:14; 5:3). The state, on the other hand, expresses its will
through laws and social conventions (4:15). Masters instruct
servants what to do (2:13-14); husbands tell wives (3:1);
church leaders inform church members, and so on (5:2).

Doing good is contrasted with doing evil. The noun
form (evil doer) occurs in 1 Peter 2:12, 14 and 4:15 but
nowhere else in the New Testament. The verb form "to do
evil" occurs in 1 Peter 3:17, Mark 3:4 (parallel in Luke 6:9)
and 3 John 11. What is doing evil? It is primarily disobeying
authority. The text in 3:8-12 also suggests a summary of evil
deeds that stem from disobedience: getting even with
others, speaking evil of others, and discord.

1 Peter 3:13—17

> Now who is there to harm you if you are zealous
> for what is right? But even if you do suffer for
> righteousness' sake, you will be blessed. Have no
> fear of them, nor be troubled, but in your hearts
> reverence Christ as Lord. Always be prepared to
> make a defense to any one who calls you to
> account for the hope that is in you, yet do it with
> gentleness and reverence; and keep your con-
> science clear, so that, when you are abused, those
> who revile your good behavior in Christ may be
> put to shame. For it is better to suffer for doing
> right, if that should be God's will, than for
> doing wrong.

Beginning in 3:13 the letter takes a turn. 1 Peter
acknowledges that difficulties can arise for the Christian,

especially for the one who desires to be obedient in all circumstances. Occasions will arise in which Christians suffer at the hands of civil authorities because of their zeal for doing what is right. When a conflict surfaces over the demands of various authorities, or when authorities demand different things, how should a Christian decide? 1 Peter is clear about this. The Christian's primary responsibility is to obey God. The priority of God applies not only to "religious" situations, but to *all* of life (1:2, 5, 14-15, 17, 21, 23, 25a; 2:13, 15, 16b; 3:15; 4:2, 14, 19; 5:6). The ethical problem at this point is: When two or more legitimate and valued yet conflicting moral demands confront an individual, how does one resolve the conflict? If obedience to God means being holy because God is holy (1 Peter 1:15; cf. Lev.11:44-45), and if honoring (taking seriously) all persons (the surrounding society) means conforming to the life of the surrounding society (2:17a; 1:14), how does one behave? Peter tells us that obedience to God takes precedence over conformity to popular social conventions and pressures.

A case of conflict that may appear more difficult to resolve is that between the commands of God and those of the state. Submissive obedience to God means following the law of the Old Testament (5:5, quoting Prov. 3:34; 3:5-6 using Sarah as an example; and 1:16 quoting Lev. 11:44-45). It may be assumed that Christians felt obligated to obey the first commandment, "Have no other gods," and the second "Have no images or idols" (figures that pretend to represent God or functioned as other deities). The Roman government, however, decreed that all persons acknowledge the emperor as divine—as god. And Rome expected compliance. Whether this was a specific conflict that developed within Peter's audience, or whether this issue was more in his mind is not certain. It is certain is that Christians were being persecuted. Even more clear is that Jesus himself had been caught in the conflict and had obeyed God (trusting in his ultimate justification by an "honest judge," that is, God: 2:23) and he suffered at the hands of the legally constituted authorities, both Jewish and Roman.

When legitimate authorities and their demands are in conflict, the ethical task is to select the more important value and then obey it. The other commands are relegated to a place of lesser importance. If the command of God is obeyed rather than the law of the state in such a situation, what was originally only an intellectual problem suddenly becomes a social and political issue: one is in trouble with the government. Apparently the government might even persecute Christians who are obedient to the government *because* they are Christians.

1 Peter 4:14-17

> *If you are reproached for the name of Christ, you are blessed, because the spirit of glory and of God rests upon you. But let none of you suffer as a murderer, or a thief, or a wrongdoer, or a mischief-maker; yet if one suffers as a Christian, let him not be ashamed, but under that name let him glorify God. For the time has come for judgement to begin with the household of God; and if it begins with us, what will be the end of those who do not obey the gospel of God?*

In this passage two problems are treated: what is the primary allegiance of the Christian? and what kind of suffering "counts" as Christian suffering? The problem of allegiance to God above all and in distinction from all other allegiances has been a central problem for the Bible from the very beginning. Eve decided to listen to her own judgement and conscience (Gen. 3:1ff); the children of Israel turned to Baal immediately upon their exodus from slavery in Egypt (Exod. 32). Indeed, the first of the Ten Commandments addresses this as the central problem. The root and the peak of sin is to turn from God to some other authority. It is the first sin; it is the paradigmatic (exemplary) sin; it is the continuing and most plaguing sin of all. In and of itself it does not necessarily "show" in specific actions; indeed there are no specific actions or deeds that necessarily accompany this sin.

However, actions eventually result. One lives a new and different life once God is ignored. This new life or these new actions could range from what we might consider very "bad" through "innocuous" all the way to "good." For example, the sin of David in seducing Bathsheba would be considered wicked today even in generally non-Christian circles, while the "sin" of the Galatians—at least according to Paul—in trying to follow the law very closely might be considered praiseworthy among most Christians. The people of Israel of the Old Testament did many things that now might be considered appropriate but which the Hebrew scriptures writers judged to be sinful. In considering actions that we might find totally irrelevant to religion today, consider the attempts on the part of the ancient Israelites to enjoy their life in the promised land. They established a monarchy, took a census, raised taxes, assembled an army, established diplomatic relations with other nations, and practiced a degree of freedom of religion. In calling all of these acts sinful, the Old Testament authors accused Israel of not obeying God in every area of life.

The point of this discussion is that the biblical writers demand that *all* of life be brought under the rule of God and that *no* other authority be obeyed. This continued to be a dilemma for 1 Peter and for the church. The problem was that a very powerful and persuasive authority, that of Romans, was competing for the allegiance of Christians. Government—local, national, whatever—is a very obvious presence. Most people acknowledge its authority. Governments tend to want total, uncritical allegiance on the part of their supporters and participants. Furthermore, unless there is a serious rebellion, most people feel fairly content with the authority to which they submit, so popular opinion tends to reinforce the government's demands. It is very difficult to criticize, much less resist, such a force. It is to Christians in just such circumstances that 1 Peter is addressed.

For Christians, Christ is the primary focus of allegiance. In some sense, the fact of reproach and persecution is a mark of God's presence. God is present where people are being persecuted and reproached for the name of Christ (v. 14).

However, suffering may also characterize other modes of life. People suffer for all sorts of reasons: physical pain, rebukes, insults, or loss of possessions or employment. But simply suffering, which is the inevitable lot of humans at some time or other, is not in itself the sign of one's obedience to and dependence upon God. Just because one is suffering does not routinely mean that God's spirit rests upon the sufferer.

Thus the author sketches a framework of causes for suffering, some of which are truly Christian, some of which are not. He lists four reasons for human suffering, none of which causes suffering that can be labeled uniquely "Christian." Murder and theft are the first two; both violate the Ten Commandments and indeed were considered by the Jews of Jesus' time to be a prohibition to all people everywhere, regardless of their commitment to the Jewish law. Murder is the worst offense. It is a violation of the sanctity of God's creation and an intrusion on the prerogative of the creator who alone can take back the life originally given. Theft is a violation of a person's rights and it threatens the security of the human community.

The next two categories are more difficult to define and understand. "Wrongdoers" are those who violate the criteria of the state, of the society, and of God. These are people who do not adhere to the will of God as it is understood in that society. "Mischief-making" sounds like an unimportant kind of problem, and indeed it comes at the end of the list. However, it is destructive to the health of society, even though it may not be illegal or in clear violation of the will of God. It falls on one end of the spectrum of those kinds of behaviors that simply are not helpful in the maintenance of human order and a happy society. There is a difference between the mischief-maker and the Christian—although the two might well have been closely identified in the popular mind of 1 Peter's time.

The Church in a Hostile World

1 Peter expresses the need to define Christian behavior for the benefit of Christians under persecution. It is also the case that persecution tended to be localized and was not the

only issue for Christians in the early days of the church. Christians needed to know exactly what behaviors could be classified as Christian and they needed to be assured that God approved of the kinds of suffering they experienced. But they also needed to know what kinds of suffering were not Christian. What is the character of the holy life that the Christian is to live in submission to God? What kinds of action are obedient expressions of God's holiness? What is "good behavior in Christ" (3:16)?

There are two sides. There is a withdrawal from worldly values: ignorant passion (1:14; 2:11; 4:2-3), malice, guile, slander, insincerity, envy (2:1), doing evil (4:15), licentiousness, drunkenness, revels, carousing, lawless idolatry and wild profligacy (4:3-4), murder, theft, mischief-making (4:15), zealousness (revolutionary activity). Then there are the positive values: earnest mutual love (1:22; 3:8; 4:8), not reviling in return (2:23; 3:9), doing good (2:12, 20; 3:11, 17), hospitality (4:9), concern for one another (3:7; 9-10), and humility (5:5).

The Suffering Church Today

The early Christians needed an adaptive strategy to help them fit themselves into a changing world. Is the same ethical outlook relevant today? If so, how is it possible? Some assume that 1 Peter is literally binding on Christians today. This view runs into the difficulty that some of its ethical provisions cannot apply. In the western world, for example, there are no longer any absolutist emperors; instead political leaders are elected. Nor is there legalized slavery. If the exhortations of 1 Peter are to be preserved in a useful manner, they must be interpreted to fit appropriately into a modern reality.

Obedience is certainly a crucial note to sound in American society in which each person desires independence and refuses to submit to others. It is difficult to have a nation or a family in which independence is the rule.

In addition, the modern world has many and diverse competing authorities. We are lured by many, coerced by a few, and constantly find ourselves in the position of having to decide whom to believe and obey. Even the seductive bland-ishments of politicians, the advertising industry, and educational systems must be seen as attempts to entice us to submit ourselves to some person or idea. These alternatives must be unmasked and evaluated. There is only one authority for the Christian: the Jesus who suffered at the hands of the very world that is trying to lure us from God.

As we consider the Christian responsibility to perform good works, 1 Peter is a good check against the tendency to follow societal norms. We must remember that works are determined to be good by their relationship to the will of God and not the will of the government or the people.

Christians of whatever era or locale, are new creatures (through the death and resurrection of Christ) and live in the light of new relationships. 1 Peter pictures that relationship as one of obedient servanthood to the just God. That model may not be in vogue today, but it is clear that each person and/or group is oriented to some particular set of values. What are they? Are they clearly recognized? 1 Peter signals that Christians have a new set of values that are expressed in obedience to God. Further, 1 Peter gives strategies for the living out of those new values. While the first century social and political institutions may no longer exist (the Roman emperor, slavery), the qualities that should pervade all relationships remains relevant: obedience and love. The particular strategies themselves may no longer be relevant, and specifics need to be provided for the demands of new authorities (governments, masters, and so forth). As far as 1 Peter is concerned, however, popular morality does not exercise authority.

Instead, the message of 1 Peter is for believers to com-mit themselves first to God, above any other authority; and second, they must sort out demands that are made upon them by many competing authorities. He challenges his readers to evaluate critically the demands of authorities. The final step is for faith to produce obedient action.

The letter of 1 Peter offers an ethic which is firmly based in a new relationship with God and which demands hierarchical obedience. God is clearly always at the top of the list. This might be called "critical obedience" since the Christian needs to sort out the conflicting authorities and needs always to remember who God is and what his will is. It also requires courage to refuse to obey authorities who are in conflict with God's will. The model of critical obedience is not an ethic of the weak who have no alternative, but of those who have chosen and accepted a new and better life in Jesus Christ.

Questions for Reflection

1. Can you give some specific instances (laws, policies, and so forth) in which local, state, or national government expresses and seeks to do the will of God? How do you know it is the will of God?

2. Does the authority of government (local, state, national, and extraterritorial agencies such as the United Nations) ever conflict with the will of God? Try to give some example, law or policy at each level of government that might conflict with God's will. How do you know the will of God—especially when it conflicts with the authority of government?

3. Obedience is the 1 Peter model of the Christian ethic. Do you prefer other models? What are they and why do you prefer them? From what New Testament or scriptural writings do your models come? If you do not care for the obedience model, are there biblical grounds for disliking it?

4. What would be on your list of "good works"? What is the source or authority for that list? What characterizes them or makes them good (love, obedience)?

5. Is suffering among any of the following groups just or unjust, Christian or deserved?
persons with cancer
political prisoners
criminal prisoners
refugees or illegal immigrants
the homeless
AIDS patients

Suggestions for Further Study

John Hall Elliot, *A Home For The Homeless: A Sociological Exegesis of I Peter, Its Situation and Strategy.* Philadelphia: Fortress, 1981. A commentary on 1 Peter; the letter is viewed as being written by the persecuted for the persecuted in the Roman Empire.

George Selwyn, *The First Epistle of St. Peter,* London: Macmillan, 1958. An important commentary in which the teaching material is meticulously examined and compared with similar material in other New Testament works.

Freeman Sleeper, "Political Responsibility According to 1 Peter," *Novum Testamentum* 10 (1968): 270–286. This article insists that 1 Peter had a political message, not simply a spiritual one, and that message needs to be applied today.

W. C. van Unnik, "The Teaching of Good Works in 1 Peter," *New Testament Studies* 1 (xxxxx): 92–110. The author concludes that good works should be understood as a general kind of humanitarianism to be directed at all people.

4

Hebrews:
The True Form of Worship

Where Duty Calls

A voice: There seems to be a real need for a day care facility in the neighborhood what with all these mothers that need to go to work.

Another voice: Mothers ought to stay home with their children.

Still another voice: Normally I'd agree with you, but these layoffs are getting worse and not many are being called back to work. Things are getting pretty desperate for some families. Even where the man is working the layoffs set 'em back pretty badly.

A voice: Do you think the day care idea might be a good one for us to think about? I know some mothers who might be interested in helping out.

Another voice: Are they members of the church?

Still another voice: I know some who aren't members who've talked about needing day care and said they thought the church would be a good place for it.

A new voice: A day care would be just one more expense for the church. Even if it paid its way it would put more work on the janitor and more wear and tear on our facilities. Our building is old and there are a lot of repairs we need to do. We have pretty limited resources, and I think we need to get our priorities straight.

A voice: I believe a top priority of the church is to try to bring help to the world.

Another voice: The problem is that the world doesn't help us a whole lot.

The new voice: It seems to me that our first obligation is to make sure the church survives. That means keeping our facilities from decaying any further than they already have. A day care program could literally destroy our fellowship area. We need a new floor, paint on the walls, and some kind of paneling on the ceiling. I think we need to attend to these urgent matters first and *then* we can start to plan for a day care or whatever the need might be . . . .

The voices go on. Does the work of the Christian focus on the religious institution, the church fellowship, the projects of the organization, and the faithful attendance to the worship of God? Is the schedule of church activities the true sphere where the Christian life is to be lived out? Or is it the obligation of the Christian to turn *outside* of the religious institutions, securities, and habits, to perform the duties of Christian love? Are the most appropriate recipients of Christian charity those who are not even within the membership or attendance of organized religious groups?

These are questions that arise constantly. Church boards face the question of how to make a limited budget meet unlimited needs in the church, the community, and the world at large. Individual Christians deal with the problem of whether to serve God within the church organization or somewhere outside of it in the "world." The letter to the Hebrews provides decisive directions in addressing this problem.

The Outlook of Hebrews

It has long been recognized that Hebrews was written to encourage Christians whose faith was weakening. Its purpose was to bring them back to the faith. This encouragement is presented in the framework of a remarkable new conception of Christianity created by the anonymous author of this "letter." It is this brilliant recasting of the traditional story of the life, death, and resurrection of Jesus into the terms of high priestly activity and sacrificial offering that is at the center of Hebrews.

This new presentation of the work of Christ often seems to overshadow the document's ethical teachings and point of view. The heavenly presence of Jesus as the High Priest and the notion of heavenly "rest" as the Christian's ultimate goal tend to place the emphasis of Hebrews on the other-worldly. This has the effect of down playing interest in the present, earthly matters, and responsibilities and opportunities of Christians. However, the writer was concerned about the present situation of his readers, and he was clearly aware that the saving activity of Jesus occurred in his earthly ministry. Modern readers are fully justified in looking to this important New Testament document for ethical instructions.

An understanding of the author's view of Christianity will be necessary if we are to describe the ethical outlook of Hebrews. It is easy to see that the main thing that has happened in this letter is a thorough and remarkable reinterpretation of the traditional story of Jesus' life and death into the story of the perfect High Priest (Christ) who offers the perfect sacrifice (himself) to achieve forgiveness for the sins of humanity. This new interpretation depends on and incorporates elements from the two thought worlds in which early Christians lived, namely, the Greek world of philosophy and the Jewish world of organized, sacrificial religion.

The impact of the Greek philosophical concepts can be seen in the author's ideas about perfection, truth, goodness, and permanence. All of these ideas are related to the work of Christ. In fact, it is only in Christ that one who seeks these ideals will find them. Their opposites are found in the world, in sin, and in human systems of religion such as that described in the Jewish scriptures and practiced in the Temple by the priests. Jesus is the mediator between the unchangeable God and a transitory humanity.

The religious system of the Old Testament, however, provides the primary background for the book of Hebrews.

The religious system found there consists of an apparatus (the Temple, priests, sacrifices) and a system (the offering of various sacrifices for sins). This setup was designed to solve mankind's problem: sin (9:28). This process was inadequate, however, because it never really completed the task for which it was intended. Neither the priests nor the sacrifices were fully effective. There was always more sin which in turn demanded more sacrifice. When one priest died, another was needed to take his place. Even the priests themselves were sinners who needed sacrifices to be made on their own behalf. But there are hints in the Old Testament of Christ's permanent solution to the human predicament of sin. Thus the author relies on the Old Testament as a blueprint of the real, true and effective means by which God deals with sin.

In Hebrews, Jesus is not portrayed as the synoptic gospels (Mark, Matthew, and Luke) present him. There he is pictured in terms of the literal details of his earthly ministry: teaching, healing, traveling with his disciples, getting into difficulty with the authorities, dying on a Roman cross. By contrast, in Hebrews Jesus is consistently described in terms taken from the Old Testament religious system—as a perfect high priest. He is depicted as human, as the priests were (2:17–18; 4:15), but sinless (4:15). Jesus' death is frequently mentioned, but always in terms of sacrifice (9:12, 14, 26; 10:19) or as an offering (10:10, 12). Though his resurrection is mentioned once (13:20), his current position is of more interest to the author of Hebrews. While Jesus is traditionally depicted as sitting at the right hand of God (8:1; 12:2), Hebrews more often locates him in the heavenly sanctuary (8:2; 9:12, 24). The clear implication is that Jesus is *now* performing his "once for all" sacrifice on our behalf. Jesus (as the perfect High Priest) provides himself (the perfect sacrifice) so that worshipers need not worry about making any more sacrifices for sins. Finally (9:28), Christ will return to earth to save those waiting for him.

On the basis of this reinterpretation, Christians can know that Jesus Christ is at this moment their savior and that his saving work is effective now on their behalf. With such an assurance, it is a simple matter for the author to exhort his readers to faithfulness.

The person and the work of Christ are unique. The absolute superiority of Christ to other beings demands that Christians take their new, saved situation more seriously. They are a new kind of community which was created through the work of Christ. He is the perfect, sinless, permanent, and unchangeable high priest who has offered himself as a complete sacrifice. This new version of Jesus' work admittedly leaves elementary views behind and goes on to "maturity" (6:1). It also involves a new use of the Old Testament. The Hebrew scriptures are viewed primarily as descriptions of a sacrificial system that has now been superseded and replaced by the life, death, and resurrection of Jesus. Indeed, all of the many Old Testament references and allusions in Hebrews point *from* the precursory Old Testament religion *toward* the perfection realized in Christ.

While most of the interest in Hebrews has centered on the innovative picture of Christ's work, the morality of the Christian life is also reinterpreted. Just as the activities of Jesus are reinterpreted as a fulfillment of the priestly and sacrificial activities, so the lives of Christians are now viewed as service or worship that is pleasing to God (9:14; 12:28; 13:16). Under the old covenant, people needed to perform sacrifices to appease God and to reestablish a relationship that had broken. Now, after the perfect sacrifice of Christ, the break between God and humanity is repaired and traditional religious sacrifices are useless and unnecessary. The repaired and restored relationship between God and humanity is still described as one of worship, but it is a true worship. Christians now extend the wholeness of their relationship with God to others through good deeds (13:16).

The lengthy early sections of Hebrews establish the idea that Christ's high priestly work has freed believers from continued sacrifices. It assures the faithful that they need not be concerned about establishing their own relationship with God through constant observation of religious rites.

Next the author turns to the immediate purpose for the letter—an exhortation to faith and action. We now turn our attention to a more detailed study of this material.

Religious Structure and Outsiders

What was the concrete life setting of the Christians whom the writer addresses in this letter? This question is not only important for a proper understanding of Hebrews, but it is also important if modern readers are to find this letter useful in their own lives.

The letter was written to exhort readers to the kind of behavior or service that was acceptable and pleasing to God. The author must have believed his readers were not behaving as they ought. There are warnings throughout the letter about the dangers which readers have fallen into or which threaten them. The list is a lengthy one. They have not paid attention to the message of truth (2:1; 6:12; 5:11); they have been led away (13:9; 6:6); their hearts have been hardened (3:8; 4:7) and they have not believed (3:12-13, 19; 4:2; 10:39). These Christians have disobeyed (4:6,11), refusing or rejecting messengers of truth (12:35); they have drifted away (2:1) or shrunk back (10:38, 39), growing weary and faint-hearted (12:3); they have not endured (10:36) or held to the confession (4:14; l0:23), and the outcome has been immorality and irreligious behavior (12:16).

Indeed, they have not clung to a correct understanding of the work of Jesus and as a result they have fallen away from their original beliefs and behaviors (cf. 10:32-39). Slipping back into old beliefs may have included reliance on established and popularly accepted religious institutions and practices. It may have meant pursuing the security promised by God through human institutions. It is clearly the author's view that their poor behavior is intimately linked to—indeed dependent upon—their lack of faith and understanding of who Jesus is and what he did. The author goes to great lengths to spell out the new reality which Jesus created and into which the Christians have been called. These readers need a rejuvenation and a maturation in their thinking about their faith; thus they are exhorted to "leave the elementary doctrine of Christ and go on to maturity" (6:1a). This is not just a call to a new life, which is radical enough. It is a call to a new mode of thought.

In the time during which Hebrews was written, the church was facing certain crises. It needed to organize itself in light of the delay in Christ's second coming. It needed to have a solid community and worship structure in order to survive in an hostile environment dominated by the Roman government. In addition, the majority of the populace did not take kindly to the Christians and their peculiar beliefs and practices. The thrust toward some form of organization can be seen as early as the New Testament writings themselves. "Getting organized" was a necessary step for the Christian community to take. There were many questions that needed to be answered. When, where, and how the church was to worship? What should be preached and taught? How should the affairs of the church be organized? Modern Christians may take the answers to these questions for granted, but these were primary concerns and tasks of the early church.

However, any time a group organizes itself, certain risks are taken and decisions made. For the first Christians and for subsequent generations there would be important consequences. Would salvation be pursued through obedience to the new, Christian system of organizing a religion? Would people rely on the organization of the church rather than on Christ? Would security be sought within the institution? Would the entrance or membership requirements be defined so narrowly that certain persons could not qualify for membership? A major thrust of the early church was its concern with the moral uprightness of those within the fellowship. Emphasizing that could mean that a person of poor reputation might be excluded. How could the growing and organizing church maintain an openness to all—even those considered outsiders?

The letter to the Hebrews confronts these problems as it examines the role of the organization (using as its prime example the organization of Old Testament sacrificial worship) and the mission of the church (using the example of the Jesus who was identified with and who died for those "outside the gate"). As the ethical views of the writer of Hebrews are examined more fully, we shall see how the author deals with these particular conflicts. They were urgent matters in the life of the early church.

The Ethics of Hebrews
Hebrews 10:12–25

> *But when Christ had offered for all time a single sacrifice for sins, he sat down at the right hand of God, then to wait until his enemies should be made a stool for his feet. For by a single offering he has perfected for all time those who are sanctified. And the Holy Spirit also bears witness to us; for after saying, "This is the covenant that I will make with them after those days, says the Lord: I will put my laws on their hearts, and write them on their minds," then he adds, "I will remember their sins and their misdeeds no more." Where there is forgiveness of these, there is no longer any offering for sin. Therefore, brethren, since we have confidence to enter the sanctuary by the blood of Jesus, by the new and living way which he opened for us through the curtain, that is, through his flesh, and since we have a great priest over the house of God, let us draw near with a true heart in full assurance of faith, with our hearts sprinkled clean from an evil conscience and our bodies washed with pure water. Let us hold fast the confession of our hope without wavering, for he who promised is faithful; and let us consider how to stir up one another to love and good works, not neglecting to meet together, as is the habit of some, but encouraging one another, and all the more as you see the Day drawing near.*

This passage is a summary of the author's views as developed in the first nine chapters. It is also an introduction to the ethical section that concludes the letter. In this summary, the work of Christ as a sacrifice for all sin is affirmed once more. The writer quotes from Jeremiah 31:31-34, saying that there is a new covenant in which there is no remembrance of sin and in which the "laws of God" will be written on the people's hearts. This reference to the laws of God signals the transition to the ethical section of the letter. Just as the Old Testament sacrificial system has been superseded by the work of Christ, so too the laws of the old covenant are replaced by an internalized ethical source.

The ethical section of the letter is introduced by the same kind of cultic language that has dominated the interpretation of Jesus throughout the first chapters. "We enter the sanctuary . . . through the curtain . . . since we have a great priest . . . let us draw near . . ." This signals a transformation of the traditional view of the Old Testament's ethical instruction. Jewish teachers, New Testament evangelists, and other New Testament writers held that the Old Testament was a resource for *torah*, or law. The Old Testament described what Israel had needed to do in the past in order to achieve the forgiveness of sins. Jesus had now taken over that former obligation and performed it for Jew and gentile alike, once and for all. The cultic worship and service toward God described in the Old Testament became unnecessary. Instead, worship and service came to be seen in terms of ethical obligations and opportunities (12:28b; 13:16b; cf. 10:19-22; 9:14b). The energy once spent by Israel through sacrificial religion to keep its place in the world could now be spent in embracing those who have *no* place in this transitory world, but who hope for rest in a better, permanent one.

Finally, there is an introduction to the ethical section stated in verses 22-25. There are two basic concerns: the first is that of keeping the faith (v. 23) and the second is that of pursuing an active and loving unity within the church (vv. 23-24.) These concerns provide the basic outline for what follows in the final three chapters of the letter.

Hebrews 11:23-29

> *By faith Moses, when he was born, was hid for three months by his parents, because they saw*

*that the child was beautiful; and they were not
afraid of the king's edict. By faith Moses, when he
was grown up, refused to be called the son of
Pharaoh's daughter, choosing rather to share ill-
treatment with the people of God than to enjoy the
fleeting pleasures of sin. He considered abuse suffered for the Christ greater wealth than the
treasures of Egypt, for he looked to the reward. By
faith he left Egypt, not being afraid of the anger of
the king; for he endured as seeing him who is invis-
ible. By faith he kept the Passover and sprinkled
the blood, so that the Destroyer of the first-born
might not touch them.*

The Old Testament contains a reservoir of *examples* for
the author of Hebrews. He devotes the entire eleventh chapter to a recitation of those examples. But notice: they are all
illustrations of only *one* thing, the centrality of faith. His list
of Old Testament faith examples provides support for the
first of the two concerns raised in the ethical introduction
(10:23). Christians are to be firm in their faith.

It is not surprising that Abraham (11:8-12, 17-19) and
Moses occupy the most space in this faith chapter. They are
two of the towering figures of the Old Testament. But also
note the way the book of Hebrews remembers and illustrates
their faith. Faith was expressed in their lives at points central
to the Hebrews writer. *Rejection* is a primary feature of life
under the will of God (v. 23c, 25, 27); and life is a pilgrimage,
a sojourn lived *outside* the camp (8-9, 25, 27).

This faith record from the Old Testament is incomplete. It
stops at about the time of the conquest of Canaan and the
establishment of the kingdom. That makes it possible for the
author to downplay that aspect of Israel's story in which the
Israelites were themselves the established authority during the
period of the Davidic monarchy. Although he does mention the
names of some of those associated with this time of worldly
power and security (v. 32b: Gideon . . . David . . .), the
mention of their activities has to do with the persecution they
suffered (vv. 35-38), and not with any exercise of their power

as leaders. The result is that the Old Testament is shown to be a source of examples for faith ("the assurance of things *hoped for*, the conviction of things *not seen*"). It is not a complete guide to the full ethical life.

In this account of Moses' life, only three incidents are mentioned. At his birth, his parents ignored Pharaoh's edict and hid Moses to preserve his life. The faith here is that of his parents; it is a faith that trusts God *in opposition to* the king. The parents chose to believe in God even if it meant placing themselves outside of the security enjoyed by those who got along well with established authority. True sonship for Moses meant the maintenance of this relationship as an outsider.

Moses himself, in faith, made the next crucial choice, that of "refusing to be called the son of Pharaoh's daughter." True sonship was not to be found in compromise with this world. That was a costly decision as it placed him outside of the comforts and security provided by the royal household. Instead, Moses chose "to share the ill-treatment with the people of God." Again, the contrast is between obeying the established political authority that provides security and identifying with God as revealed among the outsiders of this world. The writer interprets Moses' decision to distance himself from the king and identify himself with the outsiders as a decision "for the Christ" (v. 26).

Finally, it was in faith that Moses led the Exodus from Egypt. This was the culmination of Moses' maturation in sonship toward God. His total commitment to God and rejection of the securities offered by this tangible world identifies him as one of God's people. This action is again interpreted by the writer of Hebrews as a decision *against* the king (v. 27a) and *for* God (v. 27b). It is in connection with the exodus that the author includes Moses' celebration of the Passover. This reference reminds us of the theme of the first part of Hebrews where the Old Testament is a prototype of the perfect sacrifice made later in Christ. Moses' celebration of the Passover is of that same order—the celebration of a ritual whose perfection was only to come in Christ.

In this passage the Old Testament functions only as a primitive example of the sacrifices made for sin (completed in Jesus) and an encouragement to keep the faith. The Old Testament figures kept their faith in anticipation of the coming of Christ. So also the readers of the letter are encouraged to keep their faith because Christ *has* come to secure their trust. They can venture forth from the known securities of their own surroundings, whether social or religious or other securities, and meet the demands and opportunities that confront them in new and unprotected situations. Such was the result of Moses' faith; so should the faith of Christians also be.

Hebrews 12:3–6

> *Consider him who endured from sinners such hostility against himself, so that you may not grow weary or fainthearted. In your struggle against sin you have not yet resisted to the point of shedding your blood. And have you forgotten the exhortation which addresses you as sons?—My son, do not regard lightly the discipline of the Lord, nor lose courage when you are punished by him. For the Lord disciplines him whom he loves, and chastises every son whom he receives.*

The theme of this passage is *discipline*. After the recitation of the list of the Old Testament faithful in chapter 11, the author once again proceeds to give an ethical exhortation: "Therefore . . . let us run . . . the race that is set before us" (12:1). But he interrupts himself again, probably in light of what he has just recounted in chapter 11, to remind his readers that (unlike some Old Testament heroes) they have not suffered to the point of death. In any case, suffering should not be feared, because it is the discipline of God. To demonstrate this he quotes from Proverbs 3:11. This Old Testament passage provides a description of the new relationship between God and his children. The suffering that the readers do experience (or fear they might experience) is precisely how their relationship to God is to be realized.

It is important to remember that the entire cultic system of the Old Testament had been rendered obsolete, therefore useless, by Christ's work. If the routine, habit, and discipline of the temple sacrifices are no longer necessary, there is nothing for us to do. The possibility of nothing to do frightens some—and with good reason.

Some scholars believe that it was the discipline and the routine of the religious life as mapped out in the scriptures that gave Israel its character and identity as a people. These scholars feel that without some sort of discipline, some routine, some visible and tangible center, a people loses its identity and cohesiveness. They wonder how people will continue to know their own identity as a community if there is no longer a central point where they come together to worship and sacrifice and thus meet God. The author of Hebrews answers that question in his use of the passage from Proverbs. Christians will know their identity as *children*, that is, as daughters and sons of God in so far as they identify with the suffering Jesus and accept that kind of life as their discipline. Of course, the word "discipline" here does not simply mean punishment, but rather the kind of regimen that an athlete or a soldier assumes—a systematic method of training and testing that produces a powerful and skilled performer.

This prepares the reader for the author's fundamental understanding of the Christian life: the notion that worship has been transformed from religious activity into service toward the stranger. This understanding is founded precisely on the central act of Jesus in his dying "outside the camp" and so identifying with the outsiders and the needy of the world.

Hebrews 13:12–16

> We have an altar from which those who serve the tent have no right to eat. For the bodies of those animals whose blood is brought into the sanctuary by the high priest as a sacrifice for sin are burned outside the camp. So Jesus also suffered outside the gate in order to sanctify the people

> *through his own blood. Therefore let us go forth to*
> *him outside the camp and bear the abuse he*
> *endured. For here we have no lasting city, but we*
> *seek the city which is to come. Through him then*
> *let us continually offer up a sacrifice of praise to*
> *God, that is, the fruit of lips that acknowledge his*
> *name. Do not neglect to do good and to share*
> *what you have, for such sacrifices are pleasing*
> *to God.*

Here are clear ethical *instructions*. And once again, the author prefaces this instruction with a reference to the framework within which he thinks: Christ's sacrifice. The striking thing about that sacrifice is that it was made "outside the gate . . . outside the camp." It was not performed within the confines and according to the specifications of the organized religion of any society.

In 13:12, Jesus' suffering "outside the camp" supplies a moral example: since Jesus did his most important work where the outsiders lived and suffered—where this-worldly citizenship and security were not available—Christians are therefore to do the same and seek solidarity with outsiders (13:13-14). The author believes that the nature of the relationship of mankind to God is one of servant to master, worshiper to deity.

That basic relationship continues. The writer utilizes the term *latreuein* (to offer worship) in reference to the life of the Christian (9:14b; 12:28b; 13:16b). In 13:16b, for example, the term "sacrifice" is equated with "doing good" and sharing material goods with others. Christians are worshipers of God who are now able to worship truly, and this true worship takes a specifically ethical form. This is a transformation of the idea of worship from that of maintaining and practicing a cultic system for self security into the risk of venturing forth in service to those who are truly *other*. The Christian commitment is one of service to outsiders since the insiders cling to an impermanent and, therefore, false security. Ultimately, they will be shaken loose (cf. 12:26-28) and will need the security that only Christ can provide.

This transformation from ritual to service changes the ground rules for ethics. The mandate for the Christian is clear: depend upon Christ, not on anything in this world; commit yourself to those who are not secure in this world. True worship and sacrifice are found in loving and sacrificial solidarity with the outsiders of this world in light of his hope for perfection in another, better world. Such love expresses itself concretely in the sharing of goods; the outsiders are not likely to have much of this world's goods and are often in need on the most basic physical and psychological levels.

Forms of Religion: Good or Bad?

Any community of people needs to have structure and procedures on which it operates. This is clear even in very small communities such as the family. Once it became clear to the early Christians that Christ's return was not as soon as expected, they began to organize their wait for the coming heavenly rest. This meant creating structures for worship, organization, teaching, supporting the poor, and many other necessary tasks. In short, they organized to live in the Greek world. Living in Hellenistic culture was a new idea to many Christians. They saw the need to bring others from gentile and Jewish backgrounds into the church. The easy route would have been to take only those who were easy converts. The author of Hebrews cautions the early church that Christ died for all, particularly those who are least likely to find acceptance and security in the institutions of this world.

The world in which the early church took shape was dominated by the Greek language. Greek thought patterns had been spread almost universally through the conquests of Alexander the Great some 400 years earlier. This meant the task of taking a gospel message delivered by Jesus in a dialect of Hebrew (Aramaic) to an audience who could only speak and understand Greek. It was a tremendous responsibility. The author of Hebrews took a brilliant approach to such persons, many of whom were already familiar or even involved with sacrificial religions. His message to them was that Jesus has made the perfect sacrifice. You need not depend upon your own sacrifices to try to get right with God.

The process and results of "getting organized" created pressures, conflicts, regulations, and disciplines which gave the early Christians some strength in a hostile world. They needed to impress the Roman government; this they did through emphasis on living a good moral life. In stressing the morality of the church, however, Christians ran the risk of excluding some "outsiders" whose inclusion might threaten their good image. The message of Hebrews was that no religious form could adequately capture or institutionalize the work of Christ. Instead, it is precisely his work that puts an end to reliance on institutions and opens God's love to those outside the walls. As it turns out, this has been a timely warning to the church throughout its history.

For the Christian, life within the community should be characterized primarily by love. This is to be expressed concretely in such mundane ways as mutual exhortation and encouragement (3:13), service to one another (6:10) and meeting together (10:25). It is shown in more disciplined ways through obedience to church leaders (13:7, 17), the learning and teaching of true Christianity (5:12; 13:9), and sexual purity (12:16; 13:4). The sharing of material goods is a final way of serving God and showing love for one another (13:16).

This is not an ethic of those simply waiting to be delivered from this imperfect world into the coming, perfect one. Instead, there is a concern for getting along well, living in peace, with everyone (12:14), in the present. In particular, there is concern to feel and demonstrate solidarity with all of those who are abused and rejected in that same pagan world which rejected Christ (10:33-34; 13:2-3, 13-14, 16).

This is an ethic not particularly rich in detail. It is, however, clear in its direction. Rejection of the selfish and divisive attitudes and actions of the world is demanded. They must be replaced by a mutually supportive love relationship within the community, and a helpful outreach to those who are rejected by the world.

The ethic of Hebrews is one of supportive love for all, with an emphasis on solidarity with the outsider. This is viewed as man's new possibility of worship and service to God. It is an ethic designed to prevent the structures of the church from becoming so important that Christians derive more of our security from them than from Christ. It is an ethic for the time when those outside of the "camp" are kept there because the structures of the church will not allow them entrance.

The Contemporary Relevance of Hebrews

The author calls his readers to a new form of religious worship. This true worship is found in the radical lifestyle of mutually supportive love for all, especially the world's outsiders. He calls upon readers to base that lifestyle on a totally new conception of who Jesus is. This new conception of "priest" and "sacrifice" was a stunning and dramatic new interpretation for the earliest Christians; there had been no view of Jesus' work like this prior to the writing of Hebrews. The author's letter is first and foremost a radical redefinition of the way Jesus' life and ministry are considered. The author was trying to reach people who were involved in organized, ritualized religion, particularly that described in the Old Testament. He took the bull by the horns and, in effect, said: "If you like the Old Testament approach to life, to God and to religion, fine; it worked fairly well, but it was really only temporary. In Jesus we have the perfect religion, the true approach to God. Try to look at Jesus as the one who does everything that the Old Testament was trying to do—except that he does it perfectly, so you no longer need the Old Testament."

If we can understand the daring reinterpretation with which the Hebrews challenged the Christians of the first century, we may see that perhaps today Jesus must be presented in dramatic, fresh ways. This is especially true for people involved in cultic, so-called New Age, or other forms of the "new" religions. In Jesus we *do* have the perfect religion, the true approach to God. Such openness to new possibilities is undoubtedly the only way for some persons to be brought into a Christian life.

In terms of ethics, much of Hebrews is familiar. Love, purity, obedience, mutual support, even the notion of solidarity with outsiders are all lifted up. What is new is the willingness of the author to dare to place these traditional exhortations in a new framework which, he hoped, would appeal to readers who had lost their earlier vision and commitment.

There is thus a double challenge in the letter of Hebrews. First is the summons to adopt an ethic of solidarity with the outcasts of this world. Second is the invitation to redefine the work of Jesus. Christians are challenged to reach out in new ways to convey the significance of Jesus. Can security be found simply in the Christ who is both priest and sacrifice? Is it possible to feel the freedom from the ultimate confinement of religious forms, ceremonies, rituals, and institutions? Will Christians feel comfortable with "love of the outsider" as the central discipline and focus? Such is the challenge of Hebrews.

Questions for Reflection

1. How is the author of Hebrews able to do without the Old Testament as a direct source for ethical instruction? What—if anything—takes its place?

2. How can the author of Hebrews construct a Christian ethic without using the teachings of Jesus?

3. How or in what way(s) is Jesus the model of Christian ethics? What is there about him that enables the Christian to know what the moral life ought to be?

4. There is not a lot of specific ethical instruction in Hebrews. To what extent is it appropriate for Christians to resort to other, extra-biblical, ethical material to help in the articulation of a Christian ethic?

5. According to the author of Hebrews, *why* should the Christian follow or obey the ethic that he suggests?

6. The author of Hebrews reformulated the Christian tradition in radically new terms for his time and audience. Can you suggest a new reformulation of the Christian gospel—including its ethical implications—that would be persuasive and appropriate for today's reader?

Suggestions for Further Study

Helmut Koester, " 'Outside the Camp': Hebrews 13:9:14," *Harvard Theological Review* 55 (1962): 299-315. The author argues that the Christian is to take refuge in the human, not the sacred, appearance of God in the world.

T. W. Lewis, " '. . . . And If He Shrinks Back' (Hebrews 10.38b)," *New Testament Studies* 22 (1975): 88-94. Lewis suggests that the basic model for the Christian ethic is to be found in the faith community's original commitment to faith in Christ.

Alan Wikgren, "Patterns of Perfection in the Epistle to the Hebrews," *New Testament Studies* 6 (1959): 159-167. This article suggests that Jesus provides the pattern by which Christians should attempt to improve their moral lives.

5

Mark: Leave Home, Go Home

Anywhere But Here

The story is told of a pious farmer who one day saw the clouds form what he thought to be the letters "P" and "C" above his field. He took the celestial formation to be a personal message from God to him. The meaning he derived from the letters was the command: "Preach Christ!" With great excitement he began telling friends and he began to make plans to prepare for a career change. He would get out of farming and devote himself to missionary activities, perhaps even foreign missions in a faraway land.

Sometime later, the man's pastor learned of the experience and suggested a different interpretation of the heavenly revelation. His reading of the letters "P" and "C" was less exotic and dramatic; it was much more mundane and commonplace. His interpretation was that the celestial command meant simply: "Plant corn!"

The message of those clouds was nebulous at best. The different readings of the "sign" show how views of Christian service vary. For some, Christian service—living a really *Christian* life—can only happen away from home and with a total separation from the familiar environment. It consists of being dedicated to living in a culture that is completely different, often one far away. For others, the Christian life is one lived in the much more mundane and ordinary surroundings of everyday life. The gospel according to Mark emphasizes this latter approach to Christian ethics.

The Message of Mark

What is going on in Mark's gospel? Would we like to be a part of it? What kind of life does Jesus seek? The question of ethics and morality may properly be asked in these ways, rather than in terms of simply inquiring what Mark (or Jesus) wants the reader to do. Ethical concerns grow out of convictions. It is thus essential to know what convictions or beliefs lie behind the teachings derived from Mark's gospel. Ethics should be seen as responses. The reader needs to know what is taking place in the gospel in order to understand how to respond.

Jesus begins his ministry (1:15) with a short but clear sermon: "The time is fulfilled, and the kingdom of God is at hand; repent, and believe in the gospel." This sermon has two parts. In the first, Jesus announces something that is happening—the auspicious moment for the arrival of the ruling power of God. Jesus identifies himself with that event. He is part of it, and he is making it happen. The second part of the sermon is a call for listeners to respond. Jesus tells them to change their lives and to accept the new reality of God's coming reign. Mark placed this sermon at the beginning of the gospel in order to indicate to the reader what could be expected: Jesus was coming to change the world and call people into that change. The time for change is now.

As Jesus began his ministry, the kingdom (or power) of God was clearly at work. He cast out an unclean spirit from a man (1:26); he healed Peter's feverish mother-in-law (1:31); he cured many in Capernaum and throughout Galilee (1:34, 39); and he cleansed a leper (1:42). So far, so good. Jesus freely offered all of these healings; none was done in an effort to get people to behave differently or to repent of their sins. The demons were on the run and Jesus was popular with the crowds (1:28, 37, 45).

Soon, however, opposition arose. It may have been prompted by the fact that Jesus had touched an unclean leper (1:41), an action forbidden by Jewish law (Lev. 13:45–46). Or the opposition may have developed in response to Jesus' act of forgiving the sins of the paralytic (2:5). That thoroughly bothered the scribes who felt that Jesus was committing blasphemy by audaciously coopting God's exclusive prerogative to forgive sin. Other behavior which the Pharisees and scribes considered immoral soon followed: eating with sinners (2:15); failing to fast (2:18); and working (and healing) on the Sabbath (2:23; 3:5). Since the Pharisees were serious students of the Jewish law and committed to meeting the demands of that law, they were scandalized by Jesus' failure to respect those same demands. As far as they were concerned, his behavior invalidated any claim that he might be intimately associated with God or doing God's will. In contrast to Jesus, the Pharisees isolated themselves from persons who failed to fit into categories of acceptability they felt were laid down by the Jewish religion.

This brief summary demonstrates that Jesus' message and life embodied the kingdom of God. Mark's claim was that Jesus used the power of God to free people from the demonic forces and human problems that had distorted their lives. It is also clear that this liberating force met strong opposition, not only from angry demons (1:24; 5:9–13; 9:18, 29) but also from Jewish religious leaders.

What about the second part of that opening sermon, the part about repentance? It is perhaps from that portion of Jesus' message that hearers (readers) might expect to derive ethical instruction. A close look at the first part of Mark's gospel suggests that Jesus put his energies into transforming people's lives. He did the transforming. Jesus did not call people to repent as a precondition for receiving God's power, although in the process of healing he forgave their sins (2:5b). The people he dealt with did not have the energies or abilities to take care of basic medical problems. They were ill, disturbed, paralyzed. How could they have been able to go on to the more religious or spiritual task of repentance?

It seems clear that the program of Mark's gospel is to describe the work of Jesus in making people whole once again, despite the opposition of both human and superhuman forces. The question of Mark's ethic is not an easy one to answer in light of the main theme of this gospel. It is also

necessary to explore further difficulties that Jesus encoun-
tered before proceeding into the matter of Christian
behavior.

The Conflict in Jesus' Experience

The Pharisees might be considered the religious people
of Jesus' time. They viewed their task as that of studying,
teaching, and obeying the Old Testament law to the extent
that it was humanly possible to do so (cf. Ezra 7:10). They
took this task seriously as the mandate of God. Their ultimate
goal was to bring all of life under God's rule.

They also believed they ought to keep themselves away
from those things that offended God, specifically sin and the
people who were sinners. Much effort went into distinguish-
ing between what was acceptable to God and what was not.
They believed that some people were acceptable to God and
that others were not. Not surprisingly, the Pharisees placed
themselves in the first group. Those unacceptable to God
were so designated because of the quality of their physical or
moral life (such as lepers), their occupation (tax collectors),
their nationality or race (gentiles), or for any number of
other reasons.

Jesus' main objection to the kind of religion the
Pharisees practiced was precisely over this point: Jesus proclaimed that God loves everyone. Jesus demonstrated that
love by acting on God's behalf in freely healing all sorts of
people—especially those whom the Pharisees thought were
sinners.

While Jesus and the Pharisees agreed that obedience to
God should be a pervading influence in the life of each person and in the life of the community, they disagreed profoundly on how that should happen. As far as the Pharisees
were concerned, this was to occur in an exclusive and disciplined manner. Each person was supposed to make oneself over into the model of humanity revealed in the Jewish
law. Jesus, however, recognized that there were reasons why
people could not make themselves acceptable according to
any standard. The character of God is revealed in the fact

that people are divinely loved, regardless of whether they had met the standards or not. While the Pharisees sought to create a community of individuals who consciously separated themselves from others, Jesus put together a community on the basis of God's love, not human abilities and performance. Jesus wanted to include all people and he did not separate himself or his followers from anyone. By contrast, the Pharisees gloried in their exclusiveness.

This disagreement about the nature of the life to which God calls people is demonstrated starkly in the drama that unfolds in the gospel of Mark. By looking at a few representative passages, we shall see how clearly Mark describes the life Christ provides for those who accept his call and who follow him. It is a life *not* separated from the world, but intended to be lived *in* the world.

The Marcan Ethic

Mark 7:9–23

> And he said to them, "You have a fine way of rejecting the commandment of God, in order to keep your tradition! For Moses said, 'Honor your father and your mother'; and, 'He who speaks evil of father or mother, let him surely die'; but you say, 'If a man tells his father or his mother, What you would have gained from me is Corban' (that is, given to God)—then you no longer permit him to do anything for his father or mother, thus making void the word of God through your tradition which you hand on. And many such things you do." And he called the people to him again, and said to them, "Hear me, all of you, and understand: there is nothing outside a man which by going into him can defile him; but the things which come out of a man are what defile him." And when he had entered the house, and left the people, his disciples asked him about the parable. And he said to them, "Then are you also without

*understanding? Do you not see that whatever goes
into a man from outside cannot defile him, since it
enters, not his heart but his stomach, and so passes
on?" (Thus he declared all foods clean.) And he said,
"What comes out of a man is what defiles a man.
For from within, out of the heart of man, come evil
thoughts, fornication, theft, murder, adultery,
coveting, wickedness, deceit, licentiousness, envy,
slander, pride, foolishness. All these evil things come
from within, and they defile a man."*

How important for Mark's readers was keeping the
Jewish law? This passage criticizes the Pharisees and
explains to the disciples that evil originates within the
human heart. Evil is not in some other person, place, or
thing—comments prompted by the Pharisees' complaint
that Jesus' disciples did not eat with religious correctness
(7:2). Apparently the Pharisees' way of following the commandments was to withdraw into their own company. The
result was their separation from others, in some cases, even
from parents. By declaring goods or money "Corban" (or
already promised to God), the Pharisees could even evade
the responsibility of supporting their own parents. The
tradition of interpretation used by the Pharisees was a
legalistic one that resulted in separation.

Jesus' objection was not to the fact that certain
traditions had arisen, since all reading of scripture involves
interpretation and tradition. His objection was that the
Pharisees were more concerned about obeying the law than
about recognizing God's love for people. This passage points
out that Jesus expected people to adhere to the highest
ideals and most fundamental values expressed in their
society. In this case, it was the Jewish law that preserved and
revealed those ideals and values. It was important to Jesus
that people obeyed the commandments. In those commandments, the will of God guided people into healthy,
positive, and constructive relationships with one another.
The interpretation of the Pharisees produced the opposite.
The law directed people toward one another ("Honor your
father and your mother"). The law prohibited negative and

destructive relationships (theft, adultery, slander). It certainly did not prohibit people from having normal, everyday relationships required by society.

As has been pointed out previously, laws do not always fully interpret themselves. There is the constant need for interpretation. Clearly, Jesus held that the Pharisees' explanation of the law is wrong. He declares a true interpretation that represents the will of God. Jesus even claims to bring it into reality in the kingdom of God. It is not that the Pharisaic understanding was more strict. Sometimes Jesus interpreted the law more rigorously than his contemporary religionists (as in the prohibition of divorce in 10:5-9). At other times Jesus' explained the law in a more relaxed manner (as in the law against touching lepers in 1:41).

What can be learned about Jesus' ethical teachings from Mark 7:9-23? The commandments of the law are important, but the interpretation of the Pharisees is in error. They have violated the first commandment. They have replaced God with a creature of their own invention: a religion of their own efforts with walls of separation that they hope will protect them from sin. This is false religion, separating people from one another. Christians need not fear contamination from evil from any outside source, so they do not need to live a fearful and protective life as the Pharisees did.

Relationships should also be characterized and measured by avoidance of the negatives listed in verses 21-22 (evil thoughts, fornication, theft, murder, and the like). Each item in this list is something that damages others. This gives us some ideas about Jesus' defense and acceptance of the Jewish law. It is not, however, the whole story.

Mark 8:22-26

> *And they came to Bethsaida. And some people brought to him a blind man, and begged him to touch him. And he took the blind man by the hand, and led him out of the village; and when he had spit on his eyes and laid his hands upon him, he asked him, "Do you see anything?" And he looked up and said, "I see men; but they look like*

*trees, walking." Then again he laid his hands upon
his eyes; and he looked intently and was restored,
and saw everything clearly. And he sent him away
to his home, saying, "Do not even enter the
village.*

What is Jesus' picture of the good life? In this miracle
story—as in miracle stories generally—the major emphasis is
on Jesus and his willingness and ability to solve someone's
problem. In the process, he set the style or tone for the newly
healed person's post-miracle life. By looking closely at a miracle story, we find a description of the kind of life in which
Mark's readers are invited to participate. This particular story
helps us understand Jesus' vision of the world.

Several points should be stressed. First, this story is typical of Jesus' role as portrayed in Mark: that role was to bring
wholeness to people who, for one reason or another, were
unable to enjoy life fully. Jesus always worked to secure God's
richest blessings for those who had been excluded from
society for either physical or social reasons. This may be seen
in healings such as those of the leper (1:42), the paralytic
(2:11), the demoniac (5:13), and the deaf and dumb man
(7:35), among many others. Thus the first thing to
remember—and this the miracle story reminds us—is that
Jesus' task was to provide full life for each. Mark's gospel
affirms that Jesus has accomplished this goal; Mark's inclusion in the New Testament shows that the church believes
that fullness of life is still available in Christ.

Secondly, in this miracle and in others, Jesus responded
directly and appropriately to the needs of each person he
treated. He restored the blind man's sight; he repaired the
brokenness. He did not preach or merely offer sympathy; his
help was not partial. He provided repair and total restoration.
He completely removed the barrier that had kept the blind
man from full participation in this world.

A third point is that Jesus' healing was not based on the
recipient's belief in him. No recipient of his miraculous healing was required to confess faith in Jesus, God, or in any other
religious belief. Nor did Jesus heal people because they
accomplished certain moral achievements or possessed

some religious potential to be developed later. It was not just that Jesus answered people's needs, but it looks very much like he was attracted to them because they had those needs!

This passage concludes with the Jesus' command to the newly-sighted person to go directly home. This uniquely Marcan emphasis is, in effect, the reintegration of the person into his normal life. The command not to enter the village emphasizes that the return of the man to the world must begin in the most basic unit of human organization, the home. This is typical of the miracles in Mark. The restored paralytic is commanded to "rise, take up your pallet and go home" (2:11). The former demoniac is told to "go home to your friends" (5:19). The woman with the flow of blood is told, "Go" (5:34). The Syrophoenician woman went home to find her daughter freed of a demon (7:30). After people are miraculously fed they are sent away—probably home (8:10). Bartimaeus is told, "Go your way" after receiving his sight (10:52).

Not everyone is simply to "go home." But the instructions given to others immediately after their physical restoration are remarkably similar in their mundane character: Peter's mother-in-law rises from a fever to busy herself around her own kitchen (1:31b); the leper is sent off to perform the usual religious ceremonies for one cured of the disease (1:44-45, even though he does not go!); the raised girl is fed (5:43). Only once does the healed person follow Jesus as a disciple, ignoring Jesus' command to go his own way (10:52).

This view of the miracle stories in Mark gives an idea of the kind of world that Jesus desired. The stories reveal how Jesus wanted people to live. Only when this is understood can modern readers decide whether or not they want to be a part of that kind of a world.

Jesus wanted a society in which whole people, going about the necessities of life in their homes and villages, could be free from the destructive limitations of illness and social isolation. The "good life" was prescribed and offered by the community from which these people had been separated.

They could now reenter that community. It was better there than elsewhere; it was normal to be there; it was abnormal to live outside of their society. Although Jesus expected an early end to the world, Mark shows his strong commitment to life in this world. This world is where the people he encounters live. It is where Jesus himself lived. Mark portrayed Jesus at home, or going into a house on numerous occasions (2:15; 3:19; 6:4; 7:17, 24; 9:28, 33; 10:10; 14:3). Most of these references are absent from the parallel passages in Matthew and Luke; their experience of Jesus and ethical emphases differ from Mark's. Jesus did not come to create new societies, but to enable people to live more fully in their own communities.

However, did not Jesus *also* call some to leave society and to stand apart from their own culture as he did? Did not his disciples say to him: "Lo, we have left everything and followed you" (10:28)? Indeed there is this element of commitment which does seem to take those who would live in Jesus' "world" out of the world in which he found them. There is a certain tension between being rooted in society and the call to discipleship.

Mark 6:30–44

> *The apostles returned to Jesus, and told him all that they had done and taught. And he said to them, "Come away by yourselves to a lonely place, and rest a while." For many were coming and going, and they had no leisure even to eat. And they went away in the boat to a lonely place by themselves. Now many saw them going, and knew them, and they ran there on foot from all the towns, and got there ahead of them. As he went ashore he saw a great throng, and he had compassion on them, because they were like sheep without a shepherd; and he began to teach them many things. And when it grew late, his disciples came to him and said, "This is a lonely place, and the hour is now late; send them away, to go into the country and villages round about and buy*

*themselves something to eat." But he answered
them, "You give them something to eat." And they
said to him, "Shall we go and buy two hundred
denarii worth of bread, and give it to them to eat?"
And he said to them, "How many loaves have you?
Go and see." And when they had found out, they
said, "Five, and two fish." Then he commanded
them all to sit down by companies upon the green
grass. So they sat down in groups, by hundreds
and fifties. And taking the five loaves and the two
fish he looked up to heaven, and blessed, and
broke the loaves, and gave them to the disciples to
set before the people; and he divided the two fish
among them all. And they all ate and were satisfied. And they took up twelve baskets full of
broken pieces and of the fish. And those who ate
the loaves were five thousand men.*

This passage is another miracle story. There is a problem
(hunger), a solution (Jesus' transformation of five loaves and
two fish into sufficient food for five thousand men, plus women
and children), and a response (the satisfaction of the crowd
and the surplus of twelve baskets of food). But the passage is
also instruction for the disciples who had earlier (6:7) been
empowered and sent out to preach and to heal. They had done
so with great success (6:13). Upon their return, they seemed to
have forgotten the necessity of a close connection with Jesus
upon whom their success had depended. Instead, they boasted
of "all that *they* had done" (6:30).

Jesus wanted to provide for the people what they truly
needed: first his teachings (v. 34) and then food (v. 37). The
disciples, flushed with the pride of their recent successes,
told Jesus what to do: send the crowd away to buy their own
food (v. 36). Their suggestions recognized the problems
with which they were faced; but they did not turn to Jesus for
help. They relied on their own gloomy assessment of the
situation. Then Jesus asks that the disciples do a mighty work
and feed the throng. But instead of recognizing the power
that Jesus made available to them, they could only think of

the problems confronting them: there was not enough
money to buy food (v. 37).

Jesus used the opportunity to "discipline" the disciples
to look at him, not the obstacles. He showed that meeting
people's basic needs was a primary facet of the disciples'
task. This is an extension of the extraordinary healing and
teaching activity of their earlier missionary travels.

The feeding miracle reveals the disciples' lack of confidence in Jesus. He is once again the center of attention as
they watch him do what they themselves could not imagine
doing. They are virtually reduced to functioning as ushers (v.
39), waiters (41b), and busboys (v. 43)!

The performance of the disciples in Mark is uneven at
best. They are to carry on the work of Jesus, and a central—
perhaps overlooked—portion of that work is the very
unremarkable task of helping ordinary people find a full life,
whatever their local circumstances. The disciples live in
tension between the demands of commitment to the Jesus
who stands *apart from* his own world, *and* the mission to
bring healing and wholeness to people who still live as *a
part of* that very world. This is the ethical tension of Mark.
The disciple is called to depend upon Christ and is expected
to continue Jesus' ministry of wholeness on behalf of others
(3:15; 6:7–13).

Mark 10:46–52

> *And they came to Jericho; and as he was leaving
> Jericho with his disciples and a great multitude,
> Bartimaeus, a blind beggar, the son of Timaeus,
> was sitting by the roadside. And when he heard
> that it was Jesus of Nazareth, he began to cry out
> and say, "Jesus, Son of David, have mercy on me!"
> And many rebuked him, telling him to be silent;
> but he cried out all the more, "Son of David, have
> mercy on me!" And Jesus stopped and said, "Call
> him." And they called the blind man, saying to
> him, "Take heart; rise, he is calling you." And
> throwing off his mantle he sprang up and came to
> Jesus. And Jesus said to him, "What do you want*

*me to do for you?" And the blind man said to him,
"Master, let me receive my sight." And Jesus said to
him, "Go your way; your faith has made you
well." And immediately he received his sight and
followed him on the way.*

In this miracle story Jesus cures a problem that had prevented Bartimaeus from enjoying full participation in his own community. Bartimaeus was even rebuked when he attempted to secure relief (v. 48a). After Jesus healed him, he sent him on his way. However, here something different has happened. For the first time we see one who is healed and sent away turning to follow Jesus instead. This view of discipleship depicts the disciple as a person who is first made whole, then given access to full life by Jesus. This is followed by a total commitment to Jesus. As suggested previously, Jesus did not demand this commitment of anyone whom he healed. Such a commitment does not deny the goodness of the life that has been restored, or the society in which it can best function. It does recognize that the ultimate good is not found merely in one's own culture but in Jesus Christ.

Culture refers to the man-made means of survival by which all people live. It consists of all the mechanisms, strategies, and customs by which we arrange the necessities and opportunities of life. It appears in various forms which we call societies. Every society teaches its culture to its children; none of it is inborn. In the process of transmission, people are taught—and most come to believe—that the culture of their own society is the best. Certainly they are not all the same, and since each society's version of culture is different (American, Chinese, Navajo), and all are man-made, none can be equated with the will of God. Culture is a system which enables most of its members to find a fulfilling life as society defines it. Historically, no society has seemed capable of creating a culture that includes everyone. Despite the purpose of culture, no society is able to include all persons and conflicts are sure to arise both within and between societies. It seems clear that in Mark, Jesus wants each and every person to be included in this world. Instead of inventing a new, Christian culture to put people into, Jesus enabled individuals to find acceptance and fulfillment in the society that had previously condemned them to rejection.

Mark's Ethic in the New Testament Era

The Jewish religious tradition had affirmed that God wished to restore all of the world's peoples to a right relationship with himself. This was to be done through the special calling of the people of Israel. However, God did not wish to create an elite nation, or a people of outcasts removed from the world. This open, inclusive, universal tradition is flatly stated in the covenant God made with Abraham (Gen. 12:1–2). It is exemplified in the prophecy of Jonah and even more so in the latter chapters of Isaiah.

The organizing principle of the original covenant with Abraham was that God is the supreme creator, and is not to be identified with the world (as in the fertility cult religions) nor subjugated to it (as in the "fall" of Adam and Eve). The early Christians continued to recognize the supremacy and "otherness" of God with respect to this world. At first, however, they felt keenly that Christ would suddenly return and that this world would be abandoned for another, better place in heaven.

By the time Mark's gospel was being written, the expectation of an immediate return of a victorious Christ had somewhat dimmed. The church had been in existence some 30 or 40 years, and it was beginning to learn to live in this world. The energies of the church were being turned to matters of survival and long-term existence in human society. But the belief in the supremacy of God *over* this world was a real and certain one. Thus the tension expressed in Mark: on the one hand Christ came to bring the kingdom of *God*, a kingdom not identifiable with any society of this world. On the other hand, just as Christ had brought people to fullness of this life, so now the church was *in* the world and faced the task of living as believers in that world.

Mark faced this question: how do Christians live in the world but in obedience to Christ? He answered the question by showing how Jesus Christ accepted the world and its culture and enabled persons to live wholesome lives in it. At the same time, Jesus recognized that no culture could provide the perfect means for the full realization of God's design for humanity. His own rejection by Jewish and Roman authorities tragically demonstrated the inadequacy of society's ability to accept all people. Mark wrote to Christians who were persecuted by those same societies. He and they knew that God's will was not fully embodied or expressed in any culture or religion, not even the Jewish religion.

Thus there is always a tension between Jesus and the culture(s) of this world. To be a disciple—to live the full Christian ethic—is to accept the opportunities of the various cultures of the world, but never to believe that they express once and for all the perfect will of God. Christ is above culture. Discipleship means following Jesus in making it possible for people to find fulfillment in this world. The goal of discipleship is to assist persons, not to sustain or defend a particular society.

Mark's Ethic for Contemporary Christians

Most North Americans live in settings that reflect a secular culture. Whether inner city, suburban, or rural, American society has structured and organized the ways in which we live, regardless of whether we are Christians or not. There is a family (or family substitute). There are jobs: offices, farms, factories, stores. There are schools and governments. There are other groups: military services, athletic teams, worker unions, social clubs, and the like. Then there is the church. If we are Christians, do we fit into or belong to these other organized groups? Do we leave our families? homes? jobs? or do we remain in them? Often it is the case that church members not only belong to families, have jobs or go to school, but also participate in the activities of other groups such as senior citizen centers, scouting, service clubs, the United Way. All of these activities claim to contribute to the welfare of the communities in which we live.

Is discipleship merely a mode or stance of life that is lived in the ordinary setting of everyday existence as culture defines that setting? Or is discipleship a radical abandonment of the accepted cultural world. Some Christian sectarian groups such as the Amish and Hutterites have opted for this latter option. Yet if discipleship means commitment to making a full life possible for others, surely this means becoming involved in every available means to improve life for others. Exactly how this should be done remains less clear. Should one join the PTA, a service club, a fund drive? Should the disciple enter local politics? If so, how does the ministry of Jesus flow through the believer in "secular" involvements to the needy in our communities?

If discipleship means a total abandonment of this world (rejecting family, denying self, leaving homes), how are followers of Christ to perform the kind of preaching and healing ministry that Jesus commended to his disciples in Mark (6:7)? Can a disciple who is wholly separated from "the world" help the needy to find their places "in the world?" Many sensitive young persons "dropped out" of American society in the 1960s and 1970s. They may have "hit the road," "bummed around," turned "hippie," or perhaps they buried themselves in professional study or personal withdrawal. For many who have a dramatic religious experience, joining a communal group or sect group draws them physically and culturally away from their former life, friends and family. Going off to overseas mission work may appear to others to be the only acceptable life.

This dilemma is not without precedent in the history of Christianity. As early as the third century, Christians began withdrawing from their normal life situations into the desert in an effort to live better Christian lives. Within a century, the universal "Christianization" of the Roman empire (which began under Constantine in A.D. 311) saw many more Christians seeking a life of greater commitment and discipleship away from friends, families, and former life settings.

Some people have the idea that discipleship and the Christian ethic consists of doing extraordinary feats of mission service and sacrifice in exotic, far away settings. Or, for the stay-at-home Christian, it has frequently become a life of denial and abstinence: Don't do this; Don't do that. Mark questions the notions of separation and extraordinary performance as the main mode of the Christian life. We should view positively Mark's affirmation that many of the answers for solving problems and finding full life are available within the local culture. We do not need to reinvent the wheel. We do not need to go off and create a new community. Our own culture may serve us well.

The great danger with this ethical emphasis is that western Christians, particularly North Americans, have often accepted their culture uncritically. Some even come to identify Christianity and the gospel with whatever their own culture values. Jesus knew the difference between humanly produced culture and the kingdom of God. But it is often hard for *us* to resist or even recognize the temptations and pressures on us to approve just about anything the culture promotes as Christian. An American evangelist recently urged Americans to believe that the only really biblical political system was democracy and that the only really biblical economic system was capitalism. He did not seem to have noticed that representative democracy and capitalism were unknown during the New Testament era. Disciples cannot make this mistake. Disciples accept Jesus' criticism: there is always a better, a fuller, a more inclusive life than any man-made culture offers. Christians sin through culture when they cannot make room for all persons to find fulfillment.

How then does the disciple deal with the fact that culture—especially his or her own culture—is imperfect? How can one be satisfied to leave culture alone and just send people "home" to that culture? How can the disciple refrain from wanting to change that culture? The fact that Mark does not exhort his readers to changing society does not mean that Christians should overlook its inadequacies. Jesus did not do that, nor did he allow his disciples to do so. The faithful must not slip into a quietism or complacency within their culture. It may well be that society needs to change. And in some cases, it is inhuman to force people to change in order to fit society. But this is not Mark's message. Rather, he proclaims that Jesus came to heal people, not the social order.

Questions for Reflection

1. Whom does American culture exclude? Are there racial or cultural groups that do not seem to fit, particularly into the local church or community? What about convicted criminals? divorcees? sufferers of terminal illnesses? traveling salesmen? police officers? athletes? business women? drug addicts? According to Mark, what needs to be done for those who do not seem to fit the mainstream? (Not: What do *they* need to do?) How can such persons better be integrated into American society?

2. Is U.S. society actually doing for all of its members what in theory it is supposed to do? For instance, is America really a home of the free? Do Americans freely welcome the "wretched" of the earth as it says on the Statue of Liberty? How practical would that be?

3. Are there cultural arrangements that are really no good at all, that is, hopelessly beyond the possibility of providing a "home" for the fulfillment of anyone? What are they? How is it possible that they continue to exist? Are they in the U.S. or elsewhere? Are there ways in which we as individuals and/or as a nation contribute to the maintenance of these very bad arrangements?

4. Are Americans in danger of allowing society's views of what makes for the good life to become substituted for Jesus' vision as depicted by Mark? What are the points at which western values or culture defines wholeness in a way that Jesus would criticize? approve?

Suggestions for Further Study

Ernest Best, *Following Jesus: Discipleship in Mark's Gospel*, Sheffield, 1981. A full commentary on Mark which looks in particular at his presentation of discipleship.

John R. Donahue, *The Theology and Setting of Discipleship in the Gospel of Mark*, Milwaukee: Marquette University Press, 1983. Shows how Mark depicts the involvement of all sorts of people in the story of Jesus, emphasizing the notion of discipleship as entering a new "family."

John F. Kavanaugh, *Following Christ in a Consumer Society: The Spirituality of Cultural Resistance*, Maryknoll, NY: Orbis, 1981. Although this book concentrates on Matthew's picture of the Christian life, it gives a clear view of culture and a critique of U.S. society from a Christian perspective.

Arthur Koestler, *The Ghost in the Machine*, New York: Macmillan, 1967. Koestler believes the greatest human achievement is the ability to group together into societies. Humanity's failure is that the lines of culture are drawn too narrowly, resulting in conflict.

Dan Via, *The Ethics of Mark's Gospel—In the Middle of Time*, Philadelphia: Fortress, 1985. Effective use of literary analysis in exploring how the task of interpreting Mark's gospel actually forms the character and behavior of the reader.

6

Matthew: Creativity on Demand

Is There a Rule for Every Situation?

Several years ago there was a popular book, *Please Don't Eat the Daises*, which was later made into a movie. It was the story of an "average" family in which the children, who were constantly getting into difficulties, always denied responsibility for their shenanigans. They were able to do this since they had not been strictly forbidden to do certain things—such as eating the daisies from the dining room table! In my own family experience there was a child (who shall go unnamed) who stuck beans up her nose and had to be taken to the doctor to have them removed. No one had told her not to do it!

In a more serious vein, there may be many things that we ought to do and even gladly would do if we knew we were supposed to. Occasionally someone else will do something that seems like such a good idea; we wish we had thought of doing the same thing. When we do something that we should not have done, we often feel innocent when we did not know beforehand that it should not have been done. Are Christians obligated to do things that they do not explicitly know they ought to do? Are they still responsible if they inadvertently do things that they later discover they should not have done? Is ignorance of the law an excuse either for sins of omission or sins of commission? Is it possible that there could be a rule for every circumstance of life? Is guidance on every moral question that arises available?

These are serious questions that some persons have tried to answer affirmatively and then have gone on to try to catalogue directives and rules for every conceivable situation. Others have taken a different route, suggesting that since it is impossible to prescribe for every situation, people ought to "play it by ear" and simply try to do their best in each situation.

The Christian, however, is bound by the will of God. So the question becomes: Can the will of God be prescribed and spelled out for every situation? How can Christians, who continue to be imperfect, be expected to know and to do the perfect will of God? There is a temptation to resolve this tension by collapsing it in one direction or the other. There are Christians who have decided that a list can be made which faithfully represents the will of God. They attempt to follow the rules on the list, trusting that they have sought to fulfill perfectly the will of God. There are others who, recognizing the difficulties of knowing and doing the full will of God, get lazy and sloppy. They decide that the task is too difficult, and that since God is forgiving, they need not take the demands of God's will seriously. What *is* the answer?

The writer of the first gospel took the will of God very seriously. Coming from a Jewish religious background, he was familiar with the sincere attempts on the part of the Pharisees and the Essenes (at the Dead Sea community of Qumran) to study, and do the will of God (cf. Ezra 7:10). He could not record Jesus' teachings on every subject within the brief compass of his gospel. Despite that, he squarely addresses this perennial problem.

Christ Creates a Community and Puts it to Work

Jesus established a new faith community that took God seriously. That community grew out of Judaism and much of Christianity's seriousness about the Jewish law comes from these Jewish roots. The early church was a community deeply committed to God law as revealed in the Hebrew scriptures.

The first gospel has long been viewed as a guide to church organization. Biblical scholars commonly assume that it is concerned with the life of Christian discipleship and that of the community. The gospel contains more instructional materials than Mark. The picture of Jesus as a teacher or as a second, law-giving "Moses," further emphasizes that moral concerns dominate the first gospel. The fact that Matthew is seen as a guide to the Christian life is due primarily to the prominence of the Sermon on the Mount (chapters 5-7), which occupies the first "scene" of Jesus public ministry in Matthew. However, any attempt to see the Sermon as the *only* source for Jesus' teaching is a misunderstanding of Matthew's purpose. Any study of Matthew's ethic that uses only certain portions of this gospel is not an adequate study of his ethic.

The use of the narrative gospel form put Matthew in touch with the death and resurrection of Jesus in a different way than use of a letter form would have made possible. The crucifixion of Jesus clearly demonstrates the conflict of his kingdom with that of the world. Jesus' resurrection allows his continued presence within the church. This presence is the most important function Jesus has during the interim between his earthly ministry and his future coming in glory. Within this gospel framework, expanded at the beginning and the end, Matthew includes materials that show he takes the will of God seriously.

The reader is struck by the fact that Matthew inaugurates the story of Jesus' public ministry with the familiar Sermon on the Mount. It is a three chapter address consisting of some of the most demanding obligations imaginable. This sermon is an important part of Jesus' ministry. It proclaims God's expectations for creation—expectations which are far beyond the capacity of most people to achieve on a regular basis.

The Sermon on the Mount is only the beginning of Jesus' work. He continues to bring people to wholeness, to include them once again in fellowship with God and others. As Matthew progresses, we see the same Jesus who gives the virtually impossible demands of the Sermon on the Mount going on to collect disciples, and heal and forgive the needy. Finally, he was rejected by Jewish and Roman authorities. Obedience to the will of God—impossible for humans—is fulfilled by Jesus.

The conclusion of Matthew's gospel is also unique. The famed "great commission" immediately attracts the reader's attention (28:18-20) because in it Jesus appears as a teacher sending forth his disciples to teach others. The commission sums up the work of Jesus and propels it forward into the time of the church. But this Jesus who commissions is no ordinary teacher. He is one who will remain with them, available, continuing his guidance until the end of the age, however long that might be.

The fulfillment of Old Testament prophecy has long stood out as a unique emphasis in Matthew. At crucial points where behavior is the topic, the fulfillment referred to is of the "law and the prophets" (5:17; 7:12; 22:40). This legal fulfillment is something that Jesus performs. His exhortations to his disciples show that he wants them to obey the absolute will of God also. However, fulfillment of the will or demand of God is to be governed by mercy (9:13 and 12:7, quoting Hosea 6:6; also 23:23). Mercy is not readily susceptible to legal definition. When it appears in the form of a command or demand on Christians, it imposes a real burden on the imagination to come up with specific behavioral content in order to fulfill the obligation.

This brief review of the first gospel shows Matthew's understanding of the will of God. It is demanding. It is fulfilled by Jesus. It continues to exercise an obligation on the disciple. It is to be fulfilled imaginatively and mercifully. Yet Christ came in fulfillment of scriptural predictions and created a new community which he promises to be with until the end of the age. The gospel account fills in the picture of *how* that community relates to God, its sovereign.

How to Obey the Will of God

Matthew the Jew was concerned about taking the will of God seriously. Matthew the Christian knew that Jesus had changed the rules of the game so that God now accepted "sinners" and forgave them. Matthew, the disciple, prescribed a life for other disciples in which *both* the seriousness of God's demands and the responsibilities of the Christian were fully emphasized. The will of God and the responsibility of the disciple are focused in Christ because if the only emphasis is on demands, the difficulty they pose is immediately evident. Focusing only on response ignores the seriousness of the demands. A tension remains, however, evident throughout the gospels, regarding the expectations Jesus has for his disciples. They are unable to be perfectly faithful and at the same time live in a Christian community with other imperfect and sinful beings.

There is another aspect of teaching material in Matthew, the so-called "wisdom" passages. The traditional wisdom literature in the Hebrew scriptures (Job, Proverbs, Ecclesiastes) dealt with moral principles that a person could deduce from life's experiences. Some of this wisdom tradition is found in Matthew with the emphasis placed on knowing and understanding the teachings of Jesus. This material certainly harkens back to the more optimistic strains of the wisdom tradition where the concern was that God's people understand their task and practice what they had learned. The presence of the wisdom theme underlines Matthew's serious expectation of an ethical duty on the part of Christians since they are the ones who truly understand Jesus. Matthew seems to have confidence that the disciples will be able to learn what the will of God is and act upon it.

The disciples are confronted with a God who demands perfection. Yet they are clearly sinners received by God through the grace of Christ, and not by their own performance. But now they, as disciples, are expected to live a radically new life and are expected to perform up to a standard even more demanding than that held by the Pharisees.

Matthew's Eleventh Commandment Ethics—Be Creative!

Matthew 5:43–48

> *You have heard that it was said, "You shall love your*

> *neighbor and hate your enemy." But I say to you,*
> *Love your enemies and pray for those who per-*
> *secute you, so that you may be sons of your*
> *Father who is in heaven; for he makes his sun rise*
> *on the evil and on the good, and sends rain on the*
> *just and on the unjust. For if you love those who*
> *love you, what reward have you? Do not even the*
> *tax collectors do the same? And if you salute only*
> *your brethren, what more are you doing than*
> *others? Do not even the Gentiles do the same?*
> *You, therefore, must be perfect, as your heavenly*
> *Father is perfect.*

This passage is the last in a series of six sections in the Sermon on the Mount in which Jesus quotes from the *Torah* (Lev. 19:18) and then proceeds to make the law even more demanding. Instead of encouraging the love of only certain people and allowing his followers to hate or ignore the rest, Jesus increases the demands (of God) so that no one has any excuse for disregarding anyone. In fact, the proper response toward those who persecute and hate the Christians is one of love and prayer. The series of prohibitions not only against murder but even against angry thoughts toward someone; not only against adultery but even thoughts about it; not only against lying but against any oaths; not only against vengeance but against any retribution whatsoever—all these are capped off by this passage which demands a complete reversal from the ways most people respond to others.

This portion of the Sermon on the Mount culminates in the final command: "You, therefore, must be perfect, as your heavenly Father is perfect" (5:48). The Greek word here means "completed" or "mature" rather than the modern sense of perfection, yet the requirement is still high enough. This passage clearly indicates the costly stakes in Jesus' perception of God's expectations. They are extraordinarily demanding and are to be taken seriously.

We turn now to a consideration of three parables that illustrate Matthew's ethical perspective. These parables suggest that the Christian ethic is one which calls for an uncalculated, but at the same time imaginative response on the part of the disciple. But there is a real dilemma here. The demands are rigorous and the will of God exacting.

Matthew 22:11-13

> But when the king came in to look at the guests, he saw there a man who had no wedding garment; and he said to him, "Friend, how did you get in here without a wedding garment?" And he was speechless. Then the king said to the attendants, "Bind him hand and foot, and cast him into the outer darkness; there men will weep and gnash their teeth."

This brief parable of the Wedding Garment has been integrated with that of the Marriage Feast (22:1-10). The Marriage Feast tells of the invited guests' refusal to attend a most joyous occasion, of the anger of the host, and of reissuing the invitation to any who will accept. The parable of the Wedding Garment has been added to the preceding parable and tells us that, after all the guests had finally been assembled for the festivities, the king entered, addressed himself to one individual who lacked the proper attire, and asked why he was not properly dressed. He then commanded that guest to be cast out.

It is striking that the guest had not been advised specifically of his responsibility to dress for the occasion and was condemned for not having done what he had not been told to do! Matthew has included a legalistic denunciation for behavior that had not been legalistically defined. The lack of specificity in terms of behavioral expectations and the implication that it was the guest's responsibility to think of what he had not been told are the heart of the parable. It is also important to note the context into which this and the accompanying parable of the Marriage Feast are fitted. On the one hand is the happy proclamation of the coming of the kingdom of heaven to all, including the undeserving. On the other hand is the warning of judgment which is found both here and throughout Matthew.

The guest had a responsibility to act as a wedding guest, despite the total surprise of the invitation. By invitation he became something he had not been before. The guest failed to act the part and was thus removed from the guest list; his new nature was suddenly and irrevocably withdrawn.

This is a situation where the parable narratives do not tell the reader what to do. Rather they imply that one who has been received into the kingdom of heaven knows what to do. Furthermore, along with the invitation to the kingdom of heaven, a judgment is proclaimed. This judgment actually occurs in the moment of one's response to the kingdom proclamation. Thus those hearing the invitation are placed in a position of opportunity or crisis. They are responsible for the appropriate patterning of their own behavior.

The criteria for determining ethical behavior are implicit in the new person or the person's new self-understanding. That cannot be specified beforehand; the Christian ethic cannot be planned out and then handed to one upon entering. Christians have imposed upon them the demand to respond out of a new nature and in accord with the needs of the new situation.

A further specific application might be derived from the Wedding Garment parable. The guest is condemned for not responding to the needs of the king who invited him. The king, in this situation, needed to be treated as a host and in the context of the joyous wedding occasion. The failure of the guest to appreciate this points to a lack of foresight explicable only by self-centeredness. He really had not accepted the invitation to become a guest.

Matthew 25:14–30

For it will be as when a man going on a journey called his servants and entrusted to them his property; to one he gave five talents, to another two, to another one, to each according to his ability. Then he went away. He who had received the five talents went at once and traded with them; and he made five talents more. So also, he who had the two talents made two talents more. But he who had received the one talent went and dug in the ground and hid his master's money. Now after a long time the master of those servants came and settled accounts with them. And he who had received the five talents came forward, bringing five talents more, saying, "Master, you delivered to me five talents; here I have made five talents more." His master said to him, "Well done, good and faithful servant; you have been faithful over a little, I will set you over much; enter into the joy of your master." And he also who had the two talents came forward, saying, "Master, you delivered to me two talents; here I have made two talents more." His master said to him, "Well done, good and faithful servant; you have been faithful over a little, I will set you over much; enter into the joy of your master." He also who had received the one talent came forward, saying, "Master, I knew you to be a hard man, reaping where you did not sow, and gathering where you did not winnow; so I was afraid, and I went and hid your talent in the ground. Here you have what is yours." But his master answered him, "You wicked and slothful servant! You knew that I reap where I have not sowed, and gather where I have not winnowed? Then you ought to have invested my money with the bankers, and at my coming I should have received what was my own with interest. So take the talent from him, and give it to him who has the ten talents. For to every one who has will more be given, and he will have abundance; but from him who has not, even what he has will be taken away. And cast the worthless servant into the outer darkness; there men will weep and gnash their teeth.

The parable of the Talents is the only one of the three parables discussed in this chapter not unique to Matthew. It also appears, though in a different form, in Luke (19:11–27). The story tells of a man who leaves his country after having entrusted enormous sums of money to three servants. No mention is made of what the servants should do with the money; it is simply entrusted to them. Note that in the Matthean context, the parable of the Talents follows another that speaks of the unknown time for the arrival of the kingdom of heaven. That parable concludes with the warning to be watchful and prepared for the coming of the Lord (v. 13).

The real action in the story of the Talents begins when the master returns. He expresses joy over the fact that the first two servants had gained 100 percent interest on the amounts entrusted to them. One might expect that their preparedness would form the center of the story. The attention, however, focuses on the third servant who returned the precise amount entrusted to him. When the third servant buried the money he was being fairly responsible about protecting his master's money. (The Jewish rabbis of that time felt that the earth was really the only safe repository for anything.) But suddenly we discover that the master is a very "hard man" who apparently expected the servant to take some risks and capitalize on the money entrusted to him. The servant, who was not told what to do with the money and returned exactly what he had been given, is declared faithless and condemned to the outer darkness of judgement.

Since the parable is set within the warning of the imminent return of the Lord (v. 13) and the judgment that ensues (v. 30), the point of the story must be the expectation that those who have received the kingdom should respond and act responsibly and imaginatively. Rather than playing it safe, risks must be taken that could be highly dangerous. Further, the question of why the servant was unfaithful can only be answered by suggesting that he was not really acting as a servant, that is, with his master's best interests in mind. Instead, he acted selfishly in order not to risk the master's displeasure.

In the parables of the Wedding Garment and the Talents, we are confronted with the need (under the shadow of entrance into God's kingdom) to devise a particular response to a given situation. In the story that follows, it becomes clear that this response is not the result of calculated consideration but rather the natural expression of a new person.

Matthew 25:31–46

When the Son of man comes in his glory, and all the angels with him, then he will sit on his glorious throne. Before him will be gathered all the nations, and he will separate them one from another as a shepherd separates the sheep from the goats, and he will place the sheep at his right hand, but the goats at the left. Then the King will say to those at his right hand, "Come, O blessed of my Father, inherit the kingdom prepared for you from the foundation of the world; for I was hungry and you gave me food, I was thirsty and you gave me drink, I was a stranger and you welcomed me, I was naked and you clothed me, I was sick and you visited me, I was in prison and you came to me." Then the righteous will answer him, "Lord, when did we see thee hungry and feed thee, or thirsty and give thee drink? And when did we see thee a stranger and welcome thee, or naked and clothe thee? And when did we see thee sick or in prison and visit thee?" And the King will answer them, "Truly, I say to you as you did it to one of the least of these my brethren, you did it to me." Then he will say to those at his left hand, "Depart from me, you cursed, into the eternal fire prepared for the devil and his angels; for I was hungry and you gave me no food, I was thirsty and you gave me no drink, I was a stranger and you did not welcome me, naked and you did not clothe me, sick and in prison and you did not visit me." Then they also will answer, "Lord, when did we see thee hungry or thirsty or a stranger or naked or sick or in prison, and did not minister to thee?" Then he will answer them, "Truly, I say to you, as you did it not to one

of the least of these, you did it not to me." And they
will go away into eternal punishment, but the
righteous into eternal life.

This passage is commonly known as the parable of The
Great Judgment. It is not really a parable at all, but a description of the final judgment. More precisely, it describes the
criteria to be employed by the Son of Man (in the Hebrew
scriptures a heavenly figure who brings in God's reign) at the
final judgment. The saved will receive their reward because
they ministered to the specific needs of the needy (v. 40).
The damned are condemned because of their failure to act
(v. 45).

The most startling thing about this picture of the separation of the "sheep" from the "goats" is the genuine surprise of
all concerned. The sheep did not realize that they were doing
what would save them (vv. 37b–39). Their uncalculating
goodness earned them their reward, or so it seems.

The goats maintained (and most likely with the
greatest sincerity) that they had not seen the opportunities
to do the required saving deeds (v. 44). In addition, it can be
assumed that, had the goats known what would be required
of them at the final judgment, they certainly would have performed the required deeds of mercy. They would have
planned their behavior to correspond to the standards used
for judgment.

Herein lies the point of the story. Though it appears that
judgment is rendered on the basis of works, it is not a question of *actually doing* the works (which the goats would
have gladly done). Rather it is question of *how* one could do
precisely what was required, especially when the requirements had *not* been prescribed to them beforehand.
Matthew's answer to this profound question is found in the
suggestion that the standards of judgment were not law. The
answer is Christ, whose humiliation was present in the
degradation of every person's need. The only way the goats
could have responded in an acceptable manner is for them
to have known Christ, and to recognize him in the needs of
others. The sheep know Christ, thus their behavior was

uncalculated, spontaneous. They lived in response to Christ. The goats did not know Christ, or at least not well enough to recognize him, and thus they could not possibly do what was required.

This passage acknowledges a judgment of people on the basis of their deeds, but this familiar interpretation is too superficial since it does not tell the reader how one is able to do acts that are redemptive. We might go on, however, to agree with the critic who suggested that this passage presents a situation of judgment of mankind by their acts—acts which are the natural outcome of character. It is important to insist that the character which produces saving or justifying deeds is a character already reformed or remade through a prior response to Christ. Only through acceptance of the kingdom of heaven proclaimed by Christ can one behave in response to human need and give the "uncalculating help" that "gains" eternal reward.

There are three fundamental ideas which govern the use and understanding of the three parables discussed here. The first is that a person is received into the kingdom only through the prior initiative of God. Second, God expects a person to react with an appropriate response after being received into this kingdom. And third, a person's response will be measured by standards imposed later for judgment. But it also appears that these same standards are not law in the sense of prescriptive behavior, since the parables contain no prescription for behavior. Is there a contradiction or unresolved tension here?

If Christians hold to the idea that judgment is according to works, surely it would seem a gross injustice to judge them for not doing what they had not been told to do. To get off of the horns of this dilemma is not only necessary but also quite simple. It is especially so if we remember that the context of ethics is the proclamation of the kingdom. The answer to the problem is that the redeemed person is judged by the quality of their response to Jesus Christ who himself fulfilled the law (5:17b).

Jesus taught that God desires mercy (9:13; 12:7) and showed by his example that each person must respond to the needs of others as the occasion demands. The exact responses are not specified but the new nature has been specified. In the parable of the Wedding Garment, the guest is no longer just anybody. He is a wedding guest with certain obligations that ought to be willingly undertaken. The servant with two talents must risk himself for the master. The "goats" who had considered themselves "Christians" should naturally have assumed responsibility for the sufferings of others. They must all have been too preoccupied with "being religious" to realize their new nature. These parables declare and describe who one is when the kingdom has come. One is accepted and changed. The person has been given a new situation and has all the resources needed for the loving consideration of others.

There is a law of unspecified obligation which may be broken in the following manner: First, be who you now are, one received freely into God's reign. Second, you are free to risk yourself to love and help those who need you. This imaginative legalism places the full burden of ethical response on the individual in the particular situation in which he or she lives and is confronted with the needs of others. The response comes from within, from that newness of life conferred by Christ. It is to Christ, not the self, that the person responds.

The characteristic which these three parables share is the idea that the Christian is committed to an ethical response which has *not* been specified or articulated, but which will be assessed and judged. Christians are therefore placed under a certain jeopardy and called upon to use their imagination to determine the appropriate response without the aid of any clearly delineated guidelines.

Matthew in the Early Church: Getting Organized

The fact that Matthew's is the first gospel and indeed the first book of the New Testament is testimony to the importance it exercised during the formative years of the church. Many of the questions raised in Matthew are specifically "church" questions: What about paying the temple tax? Who is to have the highest seat of honor among the disciples? How should believers pray, fast, and give? What is the nature of discipleship? Indeed, what kind of a faith community was the church to be? Was it to be pure and undefiled in accord with fulfillment of the absolute will of God? Or could it be a society of many kinds of Christians, some devout, others lukewarm? The modern reader must also remember that Matthew wrote in a time when the second coming of Christ, though still expected, was no longer anticipated momentarily. It was a time when the church was separating itself from its Jewish roots—roots which Matthew took more seriously than other New Testament writers.

Matthew took the Jewish heritage quite seriously. However, he did not simply understand the will of God as a new Christian *torah*. Nor did he simply preserve Jesus' new interpretations of the ancient law, although the Sermon on the Mount does precisely that. He upheld all of these precious and useful materials *within the form of the gospel account*. Thus the Christian ethic, even for one as concerned about law as Matthew, can never be cut off from the life work, crucifixion, and resurrection of the master Jesus. In fact, in the conclusion of the gospel account, Jesus promises that he will continue *in* the church as the ever-present teacher (28:20b).

In addition to the Jewish legacy that Matthew insists upon keeping, there yet was another, more pressing difficulty that confronted the early church and held its attention for several hundred years. This was the problem of living as a rejected and suspect minority in the powerful Roman empire. The Romans had proven they could be very tough on religious groups that antagonized the government.

The gospel of Matthew served an important role in the church's efforts to survive in Rome's shadow. It did this in several ways. It provided specific rules, gave examples and encouragement, and offered prophetic proof of the truth of Christianity. In other words, Matthew had *used* the scriptures in a way that was to become a model for the church.

At the same time there was a realism to Matthew that
made it the most popular early Christian gospel. It
recognized not only that God was serious about sin and
salvation, but also that the church was full of all sorts of
people—some fully committed and some less so. Indeed,
adequately addressing the "mixed bag" of Christians across
the entire spectrum of faith and devotion was one of the
most difficult problems during the years of persecution.

So Matthew's gospel lent itself to both the theory and to
the practicalities of the church's mission during the first
several centuries of its life. He expressed the conviction that
the will of God was an absolute will, demanding allegiance
and fulfillment. He expressed the belief that disciples are
made only through the grace of Christ, and he presented the
challenge of creative and imaginative responsibility as the
ethical style of discipleship. This gospel was indeed "first" in
helping the church through the transition away from a
legalistic Judaism and toward a life and identity of its
own.

Matthew Today

Matthew's combination of realism and idealism is pertinent for modern Christians. The church still consists of many
people, all committed at different levels of intensity to the
life of discipleship. The church is still filled with people who
are sinful and who, no matter how hard they try, fall short of
fulfilling the will of God. In many ways Matthew addressed a
church quite similar to the faith communities in which
Christians today participate.

At the same time, however, Matthew took God's moral
demands as revealed through Judaism seriously—even
intensifying them in the teaching of Jesus. God is not to be
compromised. God's will is not to be watered down and
interpreted as merely requiring good intentions or mod-
erate efforts on the part of Christians. Just doing one's best
will not do. This affirmation of the endurance of God's will
forms the other polarity of Matthew's gospel. It was important when he wrote and it is still important today. Perhaps it

is even more important now since Christians live in an age of rationalism and compromise.

The two poles Matthew employs have ethical functions. On the one hand, the judgment associated with the absolute will of God reminds disciples that their own ideas and efforts are not to be identified or equated with the will of God. The recognition that the church is a mixed community is a reminder that *all* are sinners. There is no way that this tension can collapse. There is no possibility that the church can give in, forget the absolute will of God, and compromise with the world—a world that has penetrated into the church in the person of all those "sinners" on the membership roles. Nor is there the possibility of a utopian irrelevance or a detached otherworldliness on the part of a devout elite. God's reign is for all and not exclusively with those who hope to separate themselves from sinners and so fulfill the will of God.

There is yet another tension created by Matthew that is fully relevant today. The demands of the will of God, often encapsulated in law, are taken earnestly by Matthew. These cannot be compromised. Jesus himself affirms that they will not pass away (5:18); rather Jesus intensifies the demands of the Hebrew scriptures. But this is not Matthew's only position on the law. There is another position, namely the expectation that each disciple *creatively* obey the law. This is a requirement that prevents any kind of legalism from developing. The emphasis on law, in turn, keeps the creative aspect of discipleship in line with the law's objective content. Thus obedience to God's will is not simply a matter of doing something that "feels good" or that seemed to be a good idea.

It follows that the first gospel has at least two contributions to make to a contemporary quest for a Christian morality. First, it provides an identity as Christians. Persons are called freely into community by the absolute will of God and are devoted to fulfilling that will, but they recognize at the same time that this new community is in the real world, and it is not by any means perfect. Disciples have been called by the perfect fulfiller and teacher of the will of God. They are dependent upon him.

Second, there is a challenge for believers to formulate ethical lives in a manner that truly responds to the needs presented to them. This is the creative challenge. Matthew's gospel provides that challenge and tells Christ's followers that it is quite all right—indeed absolutely necessary—for them to formulate ethical responses in such a manner. This encourages the faithful to risk themselves for God, since they have already been transformed by his love. Matthew, often considered a legalist whose understanding of Jesus is simply that of a rule giver, is in fact a liberator who frees us from that unhappy picture of paralyzing, religious rules. Matthew assures his readers that they are freed by Christ—the only true fulfiller of God's will. Matthew's Christ opens for all the vistas of opportunity with the confidence that their efforts of discipleship are made within the embrace of God's love.

Questions for Reflection

1. What are some problems of the church that are not addressed in Matthew, problems that have arisen since that gospel was written? How do you work at answers for them?

2. How important is the threat of judgment for our performance of Christian ethics?

3. Is it reasonable to expect Christians to move from knowing to doing without someone telling them exactly what to do?

4. Take a problem and a proposed solution to it for group discussion (for example, war, abortion, welfare, world hunger, helping another with school work). How do those solutions arise from the new being, from your being as a Christian disciple?

5. How can such responsible creativity as demanded by Matthew be fostered in the lives of Christians and in the church in general?

6. What do you think of the Sermon on the Mount? How is it related to what Jesus does in the rest of the first gospel?

Suggestion for Further Study

Dietrich Bonhoeffer, *The Cost of Discipleship*, New York: Macmillan, 1969. Bonhoeffer uses the Sermon on the Mount as a basis for charting the ideas and behaviors of the Christian life and their relationship.

John Dominic Crossan, *In Parables: The Challenge of the Historical Jesus*, San Francisco: Harper & Row, 1973. An exciting discussion of the way to use the parables in developing Christian ethics.

Martin Franzmann, *Follow Me: Discipleship According to Saint Matthew*, St. Louis: Concordia, 1961. A full-length commentary concentrating on the relation of disciples to Jesus rather than on their actions.

John Meier, *The Vision of Matthew: Christ, Church and Morality in the First Gospel*, New York: Paulist Press, 1979. A commentary that makes explicit the moral teaching of the first gospel.

7

Luke: Stewardship

How Far Should One Go?

A teenager, the son of a well-to-do executive of a large corporation, had been chosen to give the sermon on youth Sunday. In those days he was one of the few high-school students who had his own car. The topic was the rich ruler (Luke 18:18–30). This young preacher was confronted with Jesus' challenge: "Leave all and follow me." The student's solution was to give it all to Jesus, who in turn would give it all right back! We are a people who feel a great sense of ownership of what we have and a great sense of need to have more.

"I need a drink of water," said a man as he wandered in out of the hot desert.

"I need a new stereo system," said a man, annoyed at what he felt was poor sound reproduction by the sound system he was using.

Clearly, in the one case the need seems to border on a life or death situation. In the second instance the need represents a feeling that is not as universal and certainly not life threatening. These examples are somewhat extreme, perhaps. But it must be realized that perceived "needs" in western, industrially developed countries far surpass those at the level of life sustenance in the Third World, or among peoples who lived in the distant past. In North America, people have determined that they need a great deal in order to be content. Advertising, radio, television—these media help determine what our needs should be. We need a new suit; we need a drink; we need a laxative; we need a private automobile; we need two televisions, and many other things that were thought of as luxuries only a few years ago. Our needs and the wherewithal to meet them increase every year. A recent study of the American welfare system showed that it even costs more to be poor, since the needs of the poor have also escalated.

How do we know whether we really need all the things we feel we need? Even though there are powerful media advertising messages all around us, we set the standards. We decide what we need. We determine when we have met our needs and when we have had enough. But how many of us have ever actually reached the point where we admit that we finally have *enough*?

Narrowing the focus somewhat, are the needs of Christians the same as those of non-Christians? Are their standards for choosing need levels the same? Exactly how do Christians determine their needs? When do they know they have had enough to eat, to wear, or to enjoy? How does the desire to support church institutions, mission programs, and other charitable concerns fit into the Christian's hierarchy of needs? How does the Christian allocate money to satisfy those needs?

Non-Christians might say, "When I have satisfied my needs and taken care of my own situation, then I will turn to the needs of others. After all, you can't be of much help to others if you still have problems at home." May Christians say that? May Christians devote their time, energy, and money to their own needs and only then, after their own (self-decided) wants are met, finally turn to God and others? May they as faithful disciples say, "I have only so much time, energy, and money left over after my own needs are met. God and others can have what is left."?

How does a Christian decide how much is enough? How does a Christian decide how much of oneself to devote to God? How much control ought a Christian have in the management of personal or private resources? These are tough questions that the followers of Christ cannot avoid. Fortunately, it is to questions like these that a portion of Luke's gospel is addressed.

Christ Prepares a People to Live in the World

According to Luke, the work of Jesus Christ is to be the universal savior of a people commissioned to live in the world. As universal savior, Jesus casts the net of salvation wide. Luke emphasizes the inclusion of foreigners, women, and sinners of all sorts. He even reveals a conciliatory attitude on Jesus' part toward the Pharisees. This new people, constituted by Jesus out of the ragtag of broken and rejected individuals, is forged into a new community. Their task is to live in the world, bringing the gospel to all and all to the gospel.

More than the other evangelists, Luke is interested in the setting in which the church was to live for an undetermined period of time until Christ comes again. After Luke describes Jesus forming this community, he goes on in the book of Acts to show how the Holy Spirit comes to guide this special community throughout the whole world.

The "world" for Luke was primarily the setting for long-term engagement of the new converts with an alien environment. The particular setting in which the new community lived was the Roman Empire. This was a gigantic and powerful political entity which had many good points: it provided peace and security that was advantageous for business, for travel, and for culture. In terms of religion, all varieties were tolerated. For the Christians this fact was the most terrible thing about "the world" because they could not accept the same casual view toward other religions that the Roman law took. Nor could they worship the emperor. Emperor worship was the one religion that everyone in the empire was required by law to practice, even though it was often a mere formality. The Christians had only one God and they could not compromise this in any way. Living "in the world" thus posed some exceedingly difficult problems for them.

How Much do we Give to God?

Another problem for the Christian who would be spending considerable time "in the world" was how to pay for it. In the earliest years of the new church, expectations of the immediate second coming of Christ ran high. The Christians lived on a kind of spiritual adrenalin, which can only work for so long. Eventually one must "come down" from the "high" of religious excitement and get on a more even keel. There were jobs to do, marriages to celebrate, homes to build, children to bear, and churches to organize. All of these required finances and resources of various sorts. Should the disciple give up all "worldly" resources upon joining the church? Or, is each Christian to retain personal property (or a portion of it) and manage that part privately?

This question becomes acute when one believes that the world in which the Christians live is God's world, God's creation. The material things of the world were fashioned by the creator God. The Christian is thus placed into the created world as a caretaker of God's property. What exactly does it mean to be a steward?

One difficult problem with living in the world is how to determine how much control Christians have over their own possessions. Discipleship demands a commitment. But as disciples involve themselves more in the world, they require more of this world's goods to maintain that commitment. Jesus addresses this question in the Long Travel Narrative, found in Luke 9:51-19:27. This narrative is devoted to the "journey" of the disciples—it is a kind of "pilgrim's progress" for the Christian who would live in the world, although geographically it is only a trip through the foreign territory of Samaria.

The world rejects Jesus, and the disciples learn that they are to "follow wherever . . . " (9:57). This becomes the dominant theme and organizing idea throughout this lengthy passage that is unique to Luke. The content is mainly teaching, with very little in the way of healing miracles. This passage or "trip" shows an increase in the world's rejection of Jesus as he nears Jerusalem, coupled with a call for the disciples to be more responsible in their use of possessions. The Long Travel Narrative culminates in chapter 19 with the "examples" of Zaccheus and the "faithful servants" of the parable of the Talents. This culmination emphasizes the need for serious, material devotion to a unique master. This long central passage thus connects the public ministry of Jesus (enhanced in Luke by a special emphasis on Jesus' concern for the poor and outcast) with the passion of Christ and the following history of the church in the book of Acts.

The problem appears to be a simple one. Either the disciples give up all in following Jesus, or they keep control of material goods and dispense them on Jesus' behalf. If the first course of action is pursued, the disciples end up very quickly with nothing. This may be total devotion, but is it good stewardship? If the second course is followed, the disciples still retain control. And indeed that is the problem. If the disciple may still control his or her *own* goods, how may those goods truly be considered God's and at the disposal of the master? This is the dilemma of Christians today and it has been a dilemma in the interpretation of Luke for centuries.

The Ethics of Luke

Luke 3:10-14

> And the multitudes asked him, "What then shall we do?" And he answered them, "He who has two coats, let him share with him who has none; and he who has food, let him do likewise." Tax collectors also came to be baptized, and said to him, "Teacher, what shall we do?" And he said to them, "Collect no more than is appointed you." Soldiers also asked him, "And we, what shall we do?" And he said to them, "Rob no one by violence or by false accusation, and be content with your wages."

It will be well to note that Luke takes seriously the question of responsible commitment to God from the beginning of the gospel. As this passage shows, even John the Baptist, precursor of Jesus, gave advice to all for living in this world. This included two groups of the most worldly kind of people, namely soldiers and tax collectors.

John taught the multitudes to share food, clothing, and other basic necessities of life with the needy, not with those who have a claim on the possessions or on the givers. Tax collectors are to collect, but only a fair amount. Government must be supported. Soldiers, who are in the most sensitive position of all perhaps, are given two instructions: do not extort and be content with your wages.

Such concern with material goods such as food and clothing (their possession or lack thereof) permeates the third gospel. Many figures in Luke's gospel are poor and are characterized by a lack of any claim to possessions or on anyone who has them.

Luke 6:20, 24

And He lifted up his eyes on his disciples, and said: "Blessed are you poor, for yours is the Kingdom of God . . . But woe to you that are rich for you have received your consolation.

Here are practical beatitudes (instructions that bring happiness). Note that the rich and the poor have the primary position in these teachings. In contrast with Matthew, these beatitudes are given in the "Sermon on the Plain," a down to earth setting in contrast with the Sermon on the Mount.

Who are the rich and the poor? "The poor" is a term that has both economic and religious connotations. In Jesus' day it had become a shorthand way of describing the truly or ideally religious persons of Israel. They were pious and humble people who were in a proper relation to God. The term "poor" was used more universally than "righteous" or "pious" to refer to this type of individual. The second meaning was economic: it referred to those who needed to support themselves or who depended on others for support (such as widows and orphans).

Luke drew upon both of these ideas. There is some indication that he regarded the Christian church as the reconstitution of the Israel described in the Jewish scriptures. In that sense the church was *of* the poor and *for* the poor. But his many explicit references to money and possessions indicate that Luke was also concerned about the reality of poverty and wealth, and their impact on the people who experience them.

Therefore, the poor for Luke also constituted a political and social reality that had always existed (cf. Deut. 15:11a). This condition has clearly negative overtones. It does not and will not change (7:22). To be poor means to be in the same condition as the blind, lame, leprous, deaf, and dead. There is no help for such persons. Unlike poverty in modern industrialized countries, there was no thought or possibility of upward mobility, no rags-to-riches dream that could become a reality. The one peculiar thing about poverty, however, is that it seems to depend upon the behavior of the rich. Those who have money and possessions in some way deprive others from having them.

The term poor also refers to a type of relationship. Most clearly, to be poor means to be dependent. The poor are dependent upon others and on God for whatever they obtain. The lack of resources, however, does not necessarily impose dependence upon this group. The poor are dependent because they lack any basis for a claim on those who control material goods. Thus, they lack the ability to negotiate for anything, or to repay that which is received. These features alter the structures of any relationship that the poor experience.

In contrast to Luke, the Jewish rabbis believed poverty to be a terrible condition, perhaps the greatest evil possible (cf. Prov. 30:7). The reason for this rabbinic antagonism was that poverty forced the poor into dependence upon others so that they found themselves in the same conditions as lepers, the blind, and the childless. The rabbis thus viewed poverty in relational terms, and they did

not like the character of the relationships into which poverty
forced people.

The only real point of contact between the Lucan and
rabbinic views on this topic is found in the connection between poverty and the sin of pride. Even here there is a difference. The rabbis saw poverty as the punishment for
arrogance and deceit. For Luke, one must experience
poverty in order to overcome pride.

The rabbis seemed to offer no cure for poverty. Sometimes it was felt that the wheel of circumstances would eventually turn and poverty-stricken individuals would emerge
from trouble. Sharing of property was unheard of, and the
rabbis discouraged extremism in giving alms. In Luke's gospel there is virtually no indication of which poor people
were to receive anything and how much they were to get.
Likewise, there was no follow-up on what the recipients
were to do with their alms.

In this sermon on the plain, Jesus describes two sets of
people to his disciples, the poor and the rich. In the brief
catalogue of instructions (7:27–38), he exhorts the disciples to
love their enemies. The enemies include those who want
things (a coat, other goods, loans) from Jesus' followers. The
followers are to be poor, but they are also in relationship with
the poor. The poor are also their enemies! They have what the
poor do not have, but want and need. The destructive
relationships that exist in the world exist because of human
independence from one another. These relationships are
focused in tensions between the rich and the poor—tensions
that are to be overcome by the disciples. How? By the disciples
themselves becoming poor, by becoming good stewards of
God's creation in their possessions.

"The poor" is thus a caricature of what Christians
should become—dependent, with no claims and no false
assumptions about the ability to negotiate or repay. Disciples are thrust into the position of becoming slaves or servants. If they should happen to have access to material
possessions, these must be held in trust. Christians have no
claim to them nor can they exercise sovereignty over
their disposition.

This is Luke's point: disciples are poor because they exercise no claims or rights over material resources. God alone is in charge. This leads to a new ethic. It rejects the notions of rabbinic Judaism in which poverty is viewed as a punishment and wealth as an opportunity to be charitable, thus winning God's favor. The primary concern of Jesus in Luke's ethic is that of the character and quality of relationships. Poor is better than rich because it structures relations that are more apt to be loving, of service to others, and unpretentious.

Who then are the "rich?" For Luke there are two kinds of rich. First are those who are rich in themselves (12:13; 16:19). Their material wealth is a deadend, since it isolates them when they become dependent upon it. The other kind of rich are those who are wealthy in God. This can apparently include those whose use of worldly goods, however much or little, is properly devoted to God's will. Jesus placed the Pharisees, who considered themselves to be in the second category, in the former. There is nothing of which to be proud in simply not being bad (18:11). There is need for positive action.

The rich and the powerful had been unable to protect Israel in her earlier history. The result was that the "poor" were created. The rich have a history of blunders, and so for Luke, being rich is a serious predicament. It can prevent participation in God's kingdom.

Luke 12:41-43

> *Peter said, "Lord, are you telling this parable for us or for all?" And the Lord said, "Who then is the faithful and wise steward, whom his master will set over his household, to give them their portion of food at the proper time? Blessed is that servant whom his master when he comes will find so doing."*

At this point in the gospel narrative, Luke's readers have already heard parables about helping the needy (10:25; 11:4). Later there are parables about investing money (14:28; 16:1) to derive long-term reward—not for self-benefit but as a servant pleasing the master (16:1; 17:7). Luke includes a number of these "master-servant" parables. In them, the pattern of development is typical: the master departs and returns to reward the good servant and to punish the wicked servant.

In all of Luke's "master-servant" parables, responsible servanthood is rewarded, irresponsible behavior is punished. There are no surprises. In this brief story of the faithful and wise steward, Jesus makes clear to Peter that disciples are to share two characteristics of the wise steward. Each is to be faithfully committed to doing the will of the master. And each is to wisely decide just what has to be done and just how to do it.

Luke 16:19–31

> *There was a rich man, who was clothed in purple and fine linen and who feasted sumptuously every day. And at his gate lay a poor man named Lazarus, full of sores, who desired to be fed with what fell from the rich man's table; moreover the dogs came and licked his sores. The poor man died and was carried by the angels to Abraham's bosom. The rich man also died and was buried; and in Hades, being in torment, he lifted up his eyes, and saw Abraham far off and Lazarus in his bosom. And he called out, "Father Abraham, have mercy upon me, and send Lazarus to dip the end of his finger in water and cool my tongue; for I am in anguish in this flame." But Abraham said, "Son, remember that you in your lifetime received your good things, and Lazarus in like manner evil things; but now he is comforted here, and you are in anguish. And besides all this, between us and you a great chasm has been fixed, in order that those who would pass from here to you may not be able, and none may cross from there to us." And he said, "Then I beg you, father, to send him to my father's house, for I have five brothers, so that he may warn them, lest they also come into this*

*place of torment." But Abraham said, "They have
Moses and the prophets; let them hear them." And
he said, "No, father Abraham; but if some one goes
to them from the dead, they will repent." He said to
them "If they do not hear Moses and the prophets,
neither will they be convinced if some one should
rise from the dead."*

Ethical responsibilities of the disciple include taking
the law seriously. Luke believes that the Jewish law contained sufficient information on the will of God for anyone
who studied it to know that they should use their money
(mammon) and resources to bridge human relationships. In
the story of Lazarus, the rich man should have known it was
his duty to give Lazarus food.

It must be noted that for Luke, Jesus does not intend that
concern for the poor be politically directed toward over-
turning social institutions that cause and maintain poverty.
In many passages, *giving* is the central point: 11:29, 20:35,
21:24, 28:10; and, of course, Acts 20:35: "It is more blessed
to give than to receive." According to Luke, the needs of the
poor take second place to the disciples' need to get rid of
possessions.

This is because of Luke's concern that possessions not
become a barrier to entering the kingdom of God.
Possessions do not necessarily prevent this entrance, but it is
very difficult for one encumbered with possessions to shift
concerns totally to the kingdom. Earthly possessions and
attachments are to be relinquished. This is the gospel's basic
point of view with regard to discipleship and possessions.
Second, giving to the poor means bridges are built with that
money. These bridges cannot be broken by the repayment of
any money by the poor. Giving to the poor is primarily not to
"help the poor," to "change the world," or to make oneself
"feel better." Giving eliminates barriers and obstacles that
separate the giver from others.

There is an impersonal quality to the use of money in
Luke. Its dispersal is not envisioned as having a permanent or
positive impact on the poor. Poverty and the conditions that

make for poverty will not be eliminated. In fact, if being poor
is a condition of discipleship, then giving money to the poor
would even seem counter-evangelistic, that is, it might keep
them from full discipleship!

There is, however, another function that money and
possessions play in interpersonal relationships already
hinted at. They symbolize barriers between people. The
rich man's stinginess isolates him here and hereafter
according to Jesus' parable. The Rich Fool is also isolated
from God through addiction to wealth (12:16-21); so too
is the Rich Ruler (18:23). Zaccheus is also alone, reduced
and marginalized by society (19:3). Separation is even
experienced by the not-so-wealthy as evidenced in the parable of the Pharisee and the Tax Collector (18:10-14). The
fact that the former did not practice extortion does not
render him just in Jesus' view. There must be something
more positive; there must be a removal of the barriers that
separate people. A prime example is found in the story of
Zaccheus. He promises to divest himself of four times the
amount he defrauded from others in order to return to full
relations with them. In a prudential way, the Wicked
Steward used money (albeit his master's) in order to open
relationships with others (16:1-9). Giving money away
reduces the impediments to full realization of a humanity
as God intended it to be. Giving to the poor creates
relationships which are not negotiated but instead share in
the character of God's love for humankind.

Life in the First Century World

Luke was aware that the delay in the second coming of
Christ meant that Christians would have to live in this world
for a longer period than originally anticipated. He was also
aware that the world in which the Christians had to live was
one dominated by the military might of Rome. The political
power was Rome's; the dominant cultural force, however,
was that of ancient Greece. The risk to the ethical life of the
early church was that "the world"—whether in Roman
political realities or Greek cultural forms—would come to

dominate the lives of the Christians and supply them with commonly accepted ideas of morality.

Luke's grounding of the Christian ethic in the notion of stewardship rescues it from religious legalism and cultural relativity. Belief in Christ immediately implies for Luke an ethical responsibility. The believer is drawn to Christ as a servant who is in the world which God created. The Christian does not labor for a reward. The reward is an assumed and natural part of one's relationship with God. Nor does the Christian act out of fear of punishment. In some sense it is not the servant but the Lord and Master Christ Jesus who bears the ultimate responsibility and who is all-knowing. The servant's position is a reasonable one (demanding only limited knowledge and certainly not perfection) and it provides a certain modicum of comfort and security.

The range of possibilities for the use of money given in Luke is broader than that in any other New Testament book. Of the twelve terms used by Luke to indicate uses of money, Matthew uses only eight and Mark three. Many of these terms are business terms. John the Baptist's tacit approval of tax-collecting activities (3:13) underscores acceptance of mercantile activities as appropriate for Christians. How do these uses of money and possessions relate to the more traditional categories of discipleship, entrance into the kingdom of God, and obedience to the law?

For Luke, discipleship is characterized—but not caused—by its actions. This is seen particularly in the need for giving up *all* material possessions to follow Jesus (5:11, 28; 6:20; 18:22). Luke 12:32 is verbally reminiscent of the angels' words to the shepherds in 2:14b: ". . . on earth peace among men with whom he is pleased." Verse 12:32b reads: ". . . it is your Father's good pleasure to give you the kingdom." It clarifies the basic notion that the kingdom is a gift, not part of a transaction made in response to the disciples' renunciation of possessions.

Giving up or selling of possessions *follows* receipt of the kingdom (12:33) and must be understood as the shedding of something that inhibits one who has already received the kingdom. Divestiture is a response to, not a cause for, the bestowal of the kingdom. This simply culminates a passage that urges a "carefree" and unanxious attitude on the part of a disciple (12:22). Discipleship is lived out in this mode as when Jesus sends out the seventy (10:4). Admittedly the later sending out of the disciples includes an instruction to be financially prepared (22:36). The reason is that this later passage looks forward to the time of the church and the need to equip it for life in the world. It does not change the basic view that the disciple shuns ownership in favor of dependence on the master and attention to the master's will. The long travel narrative functions as the learning pilgrimage during which the followers of Jesus learn that discipleship is stewardship (12:42). This is preparation—as the book of Acts emphasizes—for life in the world. The stewardship implied is made explicit in the way in which Luke develops Jesus' teaching on the use of money and possessions.

Stewardship Today: Pitfalls and Promises

The contemporary western world has real difficulty understanding a stewardship ethic. This is true for a number of reasons. The modern notion that people have a mind of their own and that they can decide to do the right thing with possessions is a major inhibiting factor. A second crucial factor is the notion that individuals do indeed possess or own their own goods. In view of that belief, any response to the will of God becomes an autonomous act on the individual's part. This is a quite different motivation for responding to God than the example Luke offers of the servant, a person who owned little or nothing.

A third difficulty in understanding a stewardship ethic is the assumption that Luke taught the abandonment or proper use of possessions as a prerequisite or basis for entrance into the kingdom of God. Abandoning wealth is a response, not a precondition for kingdom living. A fourth reason is that the notion of poverty is often seen as an ideal rather than a concrete ethical expectation. Related to this is the idea that the possession of goods provides a good test for a Christian's faith. Finally, the whole notion of servanthood itself is not compatible or comfortable with modern, secular values.

The difficulty of recognizing and articulating a stewardship ethic has undoubtedly been increased by the tension between the demand to give up all, and the responsibility to use one's possessions for good works. Giving up all leaves one without anything over which to be a steward, and using possessions for good works implies an autonomy of ownership and free choice in the disposal of resources. Most efforts to solve this problem result in a collapse of this tension either by idealizing or historicizing it.

An "ideal" solution argues that surrendering all is the unreachable goal and that the wise use of resources is the practical reality. This resolution leaves the disciple as a relatively independent and autonomous operator, free to impose his or her own criteria on the use of material resources. "Practical realities" justify a qualitatively different kind of ethical attitude.

The typical "historical" solution appeals to particular events and practices in the life of the church. It argues that the demand for complete sacrifice came from Jesus to his immediate followers and was confined to them only. The concession to keep, but wisely use, material resources dates from the later period of the church. Once again, the result is that the church is removed from Jesus' direct Lordship.

The idea of stewardship explains this tension without destroying it: the disciple gives up all to the master and is entrusted with the responsibility to fulfill the master's will. This includes a wise and faithful administration of material goods at his or her disposition. In dispersing or using such resources, the needs of the master *always* come first. The servant cannot first take out for his or her own needs and only then provide surpluses for the master.

It remains the case that the model most helpful for understanding the ethic in Luke is that of stewardship. Disciples live in God's created world. As servants, they are responsible to utilize all that has been entrusted to them for the purposes of their master, God.

There are a number of clear benefits that may be derived from the use of this stewardship model. For example, it relieves the servant of the need to understand all the details of the full nature of the relationship with the master. The important thing becomes to know who is in charge. This understanding shows clearly that God is in command and that the disciple is wholly devoted to the divine will. In this sense, discipleship simply means complete attentiveness to the wishes of the master. Most other questions—such as the time of the return of the master, or concerns about food and clothing—are irrelevant. The master knows the answers to those questions and cares for the servant. The ethical focus is on what one does with the master's goods.

Questions for Reflection

1. What do you *own* and in what sense do you know you *own* it? Does the belief that God is the creator and master of the universe place a divine claim on your "possessions"? How do you acknowledge this claim?

2. Consider the use of the material goods over which you have stewardship in terms of a specific problem, such as world hunger, treatment of criminals, or cost of adequate medical care. What might God want you to do to address such a problem?

3. Some people believe that a "simple life" in which as much is given up as possible, perhaps with a return to living directly off the land, is the best model for the Christian life. Do you feel that such a lifestyle is preferable? Do you think Luke would support this idea of "the simple life"?

4. If you think the Christian needs to retain control over some portion of his or her material possessions, how do you defend that position? What is the irreducible minimum that the Christian has the right to retain? How do you know?

Suggestions for Further Reading

Richard J. Cassidy, *Jesus, Politics, and Society: A Study of Luke's Gospel*, Maryknoll, New York: Orbis, 1978. A helpful commentary but errs in the direction of allowing disciples to give out of their surplus, thus blunting the clarity of demand of stewardship in the gospel.

Luke T. Johnson, *The Literary Function of Possessions in Luke-Acts*, Missoula, Montana: Scholars Press, 1977. Develops the idea that "possessions . . . are capable of expressing relations between people."

8

John: The Simple Life

Absolutely!

Young children tend to report their responses and emotions in dramatically overdrawn terms. Warm food is "boiling hot" and a fall day may be "freezing cold." Schoolmates are hated or loved. There is no middle ground, no spectrum along which to locate feelings. Parents take this to be one of the rough spots of immaturity. They hope that as their children mature they will be able to fill in the intermediate terms on the spectrum.

In between the opposites of truth and lies, good and evil, light and dark, the broad and misty areas of grey emerge and expand. In ethics there are a few absolutes, but even these muddy in the stirring of everyday situations. Is it always good to tell the truth? It is not right to kill, but are any deaths justified—say by war or as legal punishment? Are there not times when it is all right to exceed the speed limit?

Part of being an adult seems to be this ability to "waffle," to live with fuzzy thinking, to say "yes" *and* "no" at the same time. An excellent example of how this has entered into modern thinking about Christianity is found in the poem by a nineteenth century English poet, Arthur Hugh Clough, who wrote a piece entitled "The Latest Decalogue." In this poem the ability to adjust high and absolute ideals to the practicality of everyday life is given humorous but all too real expression:

Thou shalt have one God only; who
Would be at the expense of two?
No graven images may be
Worshiped, except the currency:
Swear not at all; for, for thy curse
Thine enemy is none the worse:
At church on Sunday to attend
Will serve to keep the world thy friend:
Honor thy parents: that is, all
From whom advancement may befall:
Thou shalt not kill: but need'st not strive
Officiously to keep alive:
Do not adultery commit;
Advantage rarely comes of it:
Thou shalt not steal: an empty feat,
When it's so lucrative to cheat:
Bear not false witness; let the lie
Have time on its own wings to fly:
Thou shalt not covet, but tradition
Approves all forms of competition.

The gospel of John offers a stark contrast to such fuzzy confusion. It presents an ethic that is simple: the singular focus of love. In John, love is lifted up as *the* unique characteristic of the Christian life. In this gospel love is made concrete in service and permanent in unity. There are no compromises to the Christian life possible in this understanding of Christianity. Believers are put back into the kind of simplicity that children enjoy when they can only see the world in starkly black and white terms.

For God so Loved the World

What one sees in John's gospel is a Jesus who is clearly Lord. He both embodies and reveals the love and the truth of God in the world, and he makes this love and truth available for everyone. In the first twelve chapters of John, the central focus is the incarnate or available presence of God among people in the person of Jesus. He is a divine figure who has a positive impact on the needy, and a negative impact on the traditional religious structures. Jesus is the revealer of God's will. There is virtually no discussion between Jesus and the disciples, nor are any strictly ethical commands made by him to them.

John's gospel is startling in the fact that it has excluded all ethical teaching from the "life of Jesus" and confined such instruction (with the exception of 21:15–17) to the Farewell Discourse in chapters 13 through 17. The Farewell Discourse is a common literary structure in ancient Greek, Jewish, and Christian writings. A veritable all-star list of major figures have had their last words immortalized in such discourses: Abraham, Isaac, Moses, Joshua, Samuel, David, Ezra, Steven, and Paul. In virtually every case, these final testaments contained at least some exhortations of the departing one to those who will remain behind.

Why does the fourth evangelist confine the ethical material almost exclusively to the Farewell Discourse? Because such confinement protects the ethics from association with the public life of Jesus. Put another way, the historical Jesus is not depicted as teaching or providing an example. His life work directs attention to himself as God's son, and a positive response to himself is the object of his earthly ministry. Because there is little ethical instruction as a part of that public ministry, there is little (or at least less) danger that John's readers will see Jesus as primarily an ethical teacher. Such an understanding would allow their attention to be directed away from his divine nature to the content of his instruction. The danger is that salvation might then no longer be understood as the work of Christ. If Jesus brought only ethical rules, some might falsely conclude that salvation could be achieved through obedience to those rules.

John relates the ethical teaching of Jesus to his death. Using the literary technique of a Farewell Discourse, John places ethical instruction on the threshold on events that are the culmination of Christ's work, his "hour" in 8:20, 12:23f., 13:1, and 17:1.

Whom do we Love?

While it is clear in John that God loved the whole world (3:16), it is not always clear to the disciples who it is that they are to love. The parable of the Good Samaritan in Luke 10:25–37 broadens the range of people whom the disciples should love by focusing on a person of another race and religion. But in John there is a surprising twist; it appears that love is to be directed toward other disciples only. Can this possibly be John's understanding?

While God, in Christ, can love the entire world, and while Christ can love even those individuals who may reject him, it is not possible for the disciple to express love in concrete ways to all individuals, nor is it meaningful to claim that the Christian can love the whole world. The "world," of course, is the locus of evil for John. While God's love is aimed at the redemption of a creation made by God but gone astray, the disciples are to be separated from that world. Loving the world is both dangerous and—in practical terms—meaningless.

In order to understand John's views on love, a brief comment on the nature of love is in order. Love is a reciprocal and open attitude in which people hold together and minister to each other's needs. There is both give and take. John's seemingly tough, noncompromising ethic is based on the recognition that the basic structure of relations is rooted in the nature of divine love, and that pattern is outlined in the life of Jesus. The expression of God's love for mankind in Christ caused a split; or better, those not accepting that expression of love separated themselves from Christ. Love cannot force people into a relationship—that is its unique feature. Thus the separation and alienation, the dark side of love, are an inherent (but not necessary) possibility in love. The rejection of love does not prompt hatred from the lover; instead God continues to love the world.

Service, Unity, Love

John 13:12–17

When he had washed their feet, and taken his gar-

> *ments, and resumed his place, he said to them,*
> *"Do you know what I have done to you? You call*
> *me Teacher and Lord; and you are right, for so I*
> *am. If I then, your Lord and Teacher, have washed*
> *your feet, you also ought to wash one another's*
> *feet. For I have given you an example, that you*
> *also should do as I have done to you. Truly, truly, I*
> *say to you, a servant is not greater than his mas-*
> *ter; nor is he who is sent greater than he who sent*
> *him. If you know these things, blessed are you if*
> *you do them.*

We turn now to John's ethical legacy. Like so many other examples in this gospel, this passage is Jesus' explanation of what he has done. In this case it is a *service*. He has cared for the disciples by assuming the role of a servant, with the basin and towel, and washed their feet—a then common gesture of acceptance and hospitality.

Jesus and his disciples have just shared a final meal which would be their final one together (13:2, 26). Here in John, the details of the meal are ignored and the evangelist hurries (13:2-4) to the details of Jesus' washing of the disciples' feet (13:4-12) and the accompanying discourse(s).

On the basis that he, their lord and teacher, has cleansed them, they are to do likewise to one another. Their master has now become an example. John transforms the supper into a rich, sacrificial act from which the Christian ethic is to follow.

Jesus asks the disciples to reflect on what he has done for them. Jesus' foot washing is the basis for understanding who he is in relation to the disciples. It is a simple lesson. He is their Lord. This title is used some 47 times in John's gospel, sometimes as a designation for Jesus (4:1; 11:2; 6:23), sometimes as a simple term of respect ("sir": 4:1 lff.; 9:36), and also on the lips of Peter in addressing Jesus (6:68; 13:6, 25; 21:21). It is clearly a reference to one who rules.

The other title—Teacher—requires more considera-tion. In using it here, Jesus authenticates a term which a variety of nondisciples had sparingly used throughout the gospel. It was used by two of John's disciples (1:38), by Nicodemus (3:2, 10), by scribes and Pharisees (8:4), and by Martha (11:28) and Mary (20:16). Verse 13:13 is the only time Jesus himself uses the term. What he is teaching is that service is the heart of the life of the community he has created.

Jesus affirms that it is correct to call him Teacher even though his teachings have had no explicitly ethical content. But he is a unique teacher; he is also Lord. Furthermore, Jesus is a teacher-lord who has washed the feet of his students. The reference to himself and his actions is then turned to the disciples. The command to them (v. 14) is to do exactly what he has done. It is a command to imitate Jesus' behavior. They are taught and commanded to wash one another's feet.

This is the only Johannine passage in which Jesus claims the title "teacher," and it is the most explicitly ethical exhortation. Jesus goes on to indicate that he has washed the disciple's feet as an "example" (the only occurrence of this term in the gospel of John). The command that they do as he has done is in some ways a limitation, however. It suggests a limitation of the ethical aspect of discipleship to the sphere of mutual, humble, and practical service to others within the group. There is no danger of ethics being removed from its foundation in the central work of Christ.

This opening ethical passage provides a new setting for ethical instruction, presenting a clearly defined teaching about mutual and loving service. It is a simple beginning for the ethical point of view that John develops: it gives a clear mandate to a well-defined audience, and a very down-to-earth example of what the Christian disciple does.

John 13:34–35

> *A new commandment I give to you, that you love one another; even as I have loved you, that you also love one another. By this all men will know that you are my disciples, if you have love for one another.*

Jesus gave his disciples a new commandment: to love one another. He gives this ethical instruction in the context of the announcement of his immanent departure. In the light of that tragic portent, the meaning of the command wholly escapes Peter (v. 36). Thus it appears that the command might be an intrusion into another topic, the topic of Jesus' departure. Indeed Jesus' departure is a main concern of the Farewell Discourse. The disciples are concerned about keeping contact with, and continued access to, their Teacher and Lord.

What is in this command that is genuinely "new"? This is a question that has plagued Biblical commentators. As far back in the Bible as Leviticus 19:18, God's people had been instructed to love. A review of the "new" elements in this command may help clarify the meaning intended by the author. Linguistically there are elements which occur here in John for the first time. For example, the Upper Room scene is the first time that Jesus "commands" his disciples. This passage contains the first use of the word for "commandment"; it occurs a total of 11 times in John. Each time it is found it is in connection with the command to love one another (14:15, 21; 15:10, 12). This instruction excludes (or ignores) God as an object of love. In fact, the requirements Jesus gives for discipleship exclude or ignore everything except reciprocal love among those whom he has called.

Further, the command was *given*, that is, it is a gift. Doing it was not the basis for establishing or maintaining one's relationship with God. This is supported by the following promise of continued care through the presence of the Holy Spirit (14:16). The occasional scripture verses in which human love for others seems to be a basis for God's continued love for humanity must be understood in terms of the dynamic and reciprocal nature of love. It is a kind of "chicken and egg" problem. It is foolish to attempt to demonstrate in chronological fashion whose love takes precedence in the Biblical story.

Clearly for John, the disciples are to love others because Christ first loved them. The reason why the disciples are asked to follow the law of love is new: Jesus loved and still loves them. It is the all-important reason. They are not to obey in order to achieve some personal goal or to avoid divine punishment. Their loving others is not a condition for keeping Jesus' love. John does not even suggest that such love is the will of God. The disciples may love because it is a response to the love of Christ for them.

A summary of new elements connected with this command would include the following: this community, newly created by Christ's love for the disciples, is given one decisive, all-encompassing command: love. This command finds its place at the heart of the new community's religious experience and structure. Things are new in that the life of the community is to be radically reoriented because the impact of Jesus's love for the world was radically new.

We may be surprised by the fact that this command to "love one another" seems startlingly exclusive. Is this love command intended to create and reinforce a sectarian Christian enclave, isolated from the world? There is little evidence of a universal love ethic here. John 3:16–17 refers to God's love for the world and that the world through him might be saved. Neither verse, however, speaks directly to the Christian's love for the world.

There is a difficulty in interpretation at this point. A close reading of the text suggests an in-group love ethic. Is Christian love extended only to other Christians, not the world? Has the evangelist missed a crucial element in the Christian life? Is John indeed a sectarian whose "birds of a feather" ethic may be safely ignored by the modern church while at the same time appreciating his writings for their theological and Christological riches? There seems to be a dilemma here which at best leaves the reader with a serious tension between the ethical outlook of John and that of other New Testament authors.

A brief analysis of the nature of love may help provide a resolution of this difficulty. Clearly, love is not a commodity or an action which can be quantified and measured. It implies totality of commitment, self-disclosure, vulnerability, and receptivity between and among individuals. The fourth gospel's picture of Jesus shows this commitment. He is the perfect exhibition of this aspect of love in his self-giving death. It is also fairly easy to see in Jesus' life and death his self-disclosure on behalf of humankind. The vulnerability that accompanies this self-disclosure is somewhat obscured—but certainly present—in the fourth gospel since Jesus is always pictured as a dominating figure, always in control of the situation.

Also obscured in John's account—but still there—is the fact that Jesus must be received by anyone who wishes to be illumined and redeemed. These features of love must be considered in understanding the Christian ethic propounded in John. Christians are called to commitment. Verse 15:13 implies that this might well include death, as it did for Jesus. But they are also called to self-disclosure and vulnerability. And as with Jesus, these aspects of love are apparently bound to elicit rejection (17:14).

Finally, one must receive love in order to love fully and be fully effective. Unrequited love may be a genuine emotion, but it is not nearly the complete relationship that truly reciprocated love is. The point of all this is that Johannine love must be reciprocated. This is a caution against the kind of love that would force itself on others without, at the same time, having the openness and vulnerability to receive. This is a kind of incarnational love that invites but cannot demand nor force reciprocity. Love is not a polarizing force that separates but a force that becomes fully involved without being co-opted.

Thus in John's understanding, Jesus can exhort his disciples to be in—but not of—the world. Love is not separating from the world but entering fully into it. Love is the structure as well as the character of the Johannine ethic. There is no question here of a moral dualism. Dividing the world into two and calling for a different approach to each aspect or part would undercut the ideas of creation and incarnation pre-supposed by the author. The polarization that has occurred is due to the rejection of the world. Rejection—not love—polarizes. Eleven of the twelve uses of "hate" in John have Christians, God, or Christ as the object. The last use is about the Christians hating their own lives in the world (12:25).

Another New Testament example of such "intramural" love is found in Paul who constantly uses the phrase "one another" when exhorting Christians to love and mutual submissiveness. Love needs an object (a person) and that person needs to be able to reciprocate—or to reject. Reciprocity creates community.

The immediate and serious implication of this view is that it is not possible for the disciple to have "the world" as the object of love. Love is not an action that a Christian can perform on the world. It affects the world only indirectly when the world is able to see a new community of love (already created by Christ) become visible in its own mutual loving relationships. There is no direct command to love the world; that is God's business in Christ (3:16). Instead, Jesus points out (v. 35) that the world will learn about him as it observes a mutually loving community. Clearly Jesus' love for his own world had a largely negative effect; how much less would a single disciple's puny loving effort be? The apparently exclusive love command thus takes on new meaning. It is an ethic John expects to be successful both in the formation of the new community and in witnessing to the world.

The command to wash one another's feet—a command of humble and helpful service—is here deepened and made more general in the command to love. Service, which can consist of discrete actions, delegated to others, or ritualized, is given a base in love. Service is something that needs to be done at all times. It has the features of commitment, vulnerability, and receptivity.

John 14:12-26

> *Truly, truly, I say to you, he who believes in me will also do the works that I do; and greater works than these will he do, because I go to the Father. Whatever you ask in my name, I will do it, that the Father may be glorified in the Son; if you ask anything in my name, I will do it. If you love me, you*

will keep my commandments. And I will pray the Father, and he will give you another Counselor, to be with you forever, even the Spirit of truth, whom the world cannot receive, because it neither sees him nor knows him; you know him, for he dwells with you, and will be in you. I will not leave you desolate; I will come to you. Yet a little while, and the world will see me no more, but you will see me; because I live, you will live also. In that day you will know that I am in my Father, and you in me, and I in you. He who has my commandments and keeps them, he it is who loves me; and he who loves me will be loved by my Father, and I will love him and manifest myself to him." Judas (not Iscariot) said to him, "Lord, how is it that you will manifest yourself to us, and not to the world?" Jesus answered him, "If a man loves me, he will keep my word, and my Father will love him, and we will come to him and make our home with him. He who does not love me does not keep my words; and the word which you hear is not mine but the Father's who sent me. These things I have spoken to you, while I am still with you. But the Counselor, the Holy Spirit, whom the Father will send in my name, he will teach you all things, and bring to your remembrance all that I have said to you.

In this passage, Jesus proceeds from a description of the new command to an insistence on keeping it. Occasionally, a Biblical commentator has seen here a type of *quid pro quo* in which something is given for something else. According to such a view, the disciples' love for one another would become the basis of God's continuing love of God for them.

Initially, Jesus draws the first implication of this from belief in himself: the disciples are to believe in him and continue his work (v. 12). This part of the farewell speech focuses on the disciples' Christian responsibility in the world after Jesus' departure. It was indicated previously that the work of the Christian is to believe in God (6:29). Certainly it is made plain throughout the gospel that this was Jesus' primary focus. However, there is also a specific command to ethical action. Jesus' task was to gather his own to himself. This work will continue on the basis of the service and love which becomes visible to the world in and through the disciples. This can produce even "greater works" as the unity of the Father and Son is more fully realized (v. 12).

Are miracles such as Jesus performed to be a part of the disciples' "greater works"? John's answer is no. The miracle stories are systematically down-played in the fourth gospel. Miraculous signs are not the way by which the world recognizes Christ. The disciples do not have a mandate to perform such phenomena. The "greater works" referred to are not miracles but the practice of love and the impact that a loving community can have on the world in which it lives. That love is possible because of the more perfect relationship to Christ and God.

The next two verses contain a version of a traditional saying:

Whatever you ask in my name, I will do it.
If you ask (me) anything in my name, I will do it.

These also appear in the synoptic gospels in other contexts, as well as elsewhere in John:

Whatever you ask the Father in my name, he may give it to you. (15:6)

If you ask anything of the Father, he will give it to you in my name. (16:23)

John uses this saying consistently in contexts for ethical instruction. Here Jesus guarantees that he will perform whatever is necessary for disciples to do the "greater works" that he expects. This lifts up another important element, namely that the ethical life of the disciples is not merely commanded but is given and strengthened by Jesus.

Keeping the commandment(s) emerges from the disciples' love of Christ. It is made possible by the continuing love of Christ who will provide for the disciples in the future through a "Counselor." The Counselor is described in terms of his relationship to the world (by which he is rejected) and to the disciples (by whom he is recognized). These two relationships convey little in terms of ethics, but they certainly establish that the recipients of the Counselor's care are clearly in God's care. The Counselor tells more about Christ's continuing assurance of accessibility to the disciples than about the ethical content of their mission. The "historical" Jesus of the gospel narrative will continue to love and spiritually lead the disciples.

Verse 21 returns to the nature of the relationship between Christ of those keeping the commandments. It is a mutually interrelating relationship of love which binds ever closer. Stressing the love relationship, which John portrays as dynamically interrelated, is more important than specifying particulars. Keeping Christ's commands is another way of depicting the mutual interrelatedness between the disciples and their Lord.

The coming revelation (in the death and resurrection) will not be acceptable to the world, but only to the disciples. The world may then be shut off from God again. But God and Christ will come to those who obey the command to love (v. 23) or maintain the new covenantal stipulations. The community will bear the total weight of representing God in and to the world. For John, Christian ethics are identical to the mission of the church in the world. The final words of Jesus in this passage (vv. 23–24) do not make God's love for persons dependent on loving Christ or keeping God's word. As indicated earlier, love becomes a mutually reinforcing relationship that soon is impossible to analyze, calculate, and sequence.

Finally, the Counselor or Holy Spirit is mentioned again (v. 26) with its function: to teach all things, and bring to remembrance all that Jesus said to the disciples. The church will use Jesus' teaching to give content to the ethical life. These teachings were not all recorded in John. Many of them are found in the other gospels. As noted earlier, John did not include explicitly ethical materials in order to avoid the

impression that Jesus' main work was to teach people how
to behave.

What the reader sees in this passage is the need for the
disciple to be close to Jesus (and his words) and through
him, close to God. This is enabled first, by God being in
Christ who loves people; second, by the promise of the
Counselor; and third, by the encouragement to ask (pray) for
anything necessary for the Christian life and mission. The
resources for ethics are made abundantly clear in this portion of Jesus' legacy. God does not leave humankind on its
own because he loves us. The world needs people to make a
clear witness of God's love through the new loving relationships.

John 17:20–26

> *I do not pray for these only, but also for those who
> believe in me through their word, that they may all
> be one; even as thou, Father, art in me, and I in
> thee, that they also may be in us, so that the world
> may believe that thou hast sent me. The glory
> which thou hast given me I have given to them,
> that they may be one even as we are one, I in them
> and thou in me, that they may become perfectly
> one, so that the world may know that thou hast
> sent me and hast loved them even as thou hast
> loved me. Father, I desire that they also, whom
> thou hast given me, may be with me where I am, to
> behold my glory which thou hast given me in thy
> love for me before the foundation of the world. O
> righteous Father, the world has not known thee,
> but I have known thee; and these know that thou
> hast sent me. I made known to them thy name,
> and I will make it known, that the love with which
> thou hast loved me may be in them, and I in
> them.*

Disciples have been given the command to love, illustrated by Jesus in actions of love and service. This passage
gives the third and deepest layer of John's ethical legacy. This
is the structure of love. Here is a high priestly prayer for the

unity of the church. It is not primarily an ethical exhortation, nor is it ecumenical or organizational. It is directed not to the church but to the Father, although the disciples "listen in." It is a prayer on behalf of those disciples and on behalf of others yet to come (v. 20).

It is important to note again, as in the previously discussed passages, that the disciples have been placed in their present position by a power outside of themselves. God has given them to Jesus (v. 6); they have been separated from the world and identified with Jesus and the Father. They are approaching a crisis in Jesus's nearing arrest, trial, and crucifixion. It is a crisis that will characterize the church from this point on into the future.

In the Farewell Discourse, Jesus prepared the disciples for his departure. A number of problems will arise when Jesus is gone: How can anyone believe in him without seeing him as the disciples had? How will anyone be able to experience his love without his presence? Exhortations on his behalf and efforts on the part of the disciples will not be sufficient to keep them from the world and the "evil one" (v. 15). Thus these final words of Jesus are a prayer that God might establish the solidarity and security of the disciples (vv. 9, 11, 15, 20). This prayer consists of a number of steps. It is offered on behalf of those given to Christ (v. 9), not on behalf of "the world." Jesus prays that they be "kept" (vv. 11, 15) and not taken away from or out of the world; that they have joy (v. 13); that truth sanctify them (v. 16); and that they become one (vv. 20, 23) with Christ (v. 24). The effect of this oneness, as the earlier effect of love, is that the world may believe that all this originated with the creator God (v. 21).

Love may be the emotion and energy motivating the disciples in the proper ethical direction, but it is not sufficient. Love must be expressed concretely in service. But service, to be a continuing and visible reality, must have a stable context. What is necessary for the disciples' security and for the actual performance of their mission is unity or oneness. These disciples—and others who will come along—need to be formed into one totality. They need a structural framework that establishes love as something serious and enduring. They need a community to incarnate love, to make it actual, visible, and social. Christ's church will certainly have differences, if only the differences between the "these" and the "those" of verse 20. But the church's mission will be accomplished only when God's love is clearly manifested in visible form. While that form is not something John undertakes to describe, it is certain that there must be a concrete reality conveying the loving service of Christ in the world.

Why does John not specify the form? The form itself is not important. What is important is that there be some visible expression of unity so that love can express itself concretely in service. Incarnational love, God in Christ, makes it possible for Christ to express himself concretely in service to the world. Such a love is clearly beyond the capacity of the disciples to create on their own. It is a "perfect unity" (John's only use of "perfect" occurs here in v. 23). The disciples need to know that God's love is a gift. They need also to hear that Christ is praying that the gift be given. As they have been instructed to ask for whatever they need to fulfill the love command, now they hear Jesus asking for that which is necessary: unity. The intimacy of the relationships between Christ and the disciples is also described in terms of knowledge. Knowledge or understanding will be an important factor in the future working out of the love ethic.

The outcome of Jesus' prayer should be knowledge. The world will see the church's "perfect unity" (v. 23) and the disciples will have the ongoing knowledge of God's name and love. The world cannot know Christ directly and is, from now on, dependent on the perfection of the church in order to see that love. This is a tremendously heavy burden placed upon the church. Ethics indeed takes on a new function. The world's only true knowledge of Jesus is through the loving service performed within the unity of the church. Unity provides a structure, a time, and a place, in which love can be expressed in concrete service.

The sequence of John's ethic developed to this point is this: love and service are exemplified in Jesus. Service is an expression of love. Love is also the intended relationship between God and humankind. Yet it must produce a concrete and perfect unity in order to be the true expression of divine will. The Farewell Discourse leads through these apparently simple ideas from one to the next until there is a complete Johannine picture of the Christian life. Love, service, and unity point to an ethical life that is *simple* in the sense that it anticipates concrete and uncompromising expression. This love is undiluted by compromise or by the addition of other ethical concerns, principles, or demands. It is simple in its focus, but not in ease of execution.

After Jesus is Gone

One of the major concerns in John's gospel is to prepare the church for its mission in the time after Jesus has departed. John was not interested in problems related to the state (1 Peter), or the organization of the church (Matthew), but to the intimate relationship of the believer's faith in Christ. In a nutshell, how could faith be attained in the Jesus whom God sent to love the world, if that "historical" and visible Jesus were not in this world and directly accessible to potential believers? Another passage from John suggests the ethic for a church that is in the world without the person of Jesus.

John 21:15–17

> *When they had finished breakfast, Jesus said to Simon Peter, "Simon, son of John, do you love me more than these?" He said to him, "Yes, Lord; you know that I love you." He said to him, "Feed my lambs." A second time he said to him, "Simon, son of John, do you love me?" He said to him, "Yes, Lord; you know that I love you." He said to him, "Tend my sheep." He said to him the third time, "Simon, son of John, do you love me?" Peter was grieved because he said to him the third time, "Do you love me?" And he said to him, "Lord, you know everything; you know that I love you." Jesus said to him, "Feed my sheep."*

These words of Jesus have many similarities with the ethic already revealed in the body of John's gospel. Here the risen Jesus has returned (in a sacramental setting—the eating of a meal) and he reaffirms that he is always present and available regardless of circumstances. More specifically, he establishes the identity between the Jesus who lived as a man with the risen Christ gone to live with the Father and replaced by the Holy Spirit.

After the departure of Jesus, a new era of history began. The church to which John wrote needed to know that its life was to be the same ethically as before the death and resurrection of Jesus. The risen Lord presented the same description and mandate as had the living and earthly Lord: service, love, and unity. The ethic for those who came later was the same as for those who had come before. Jesus was equally available to the "latecomers" as he was to the original disciples! This passage shows that the resurrected Jesus simply reaffirmed the ethic he delivered to the disciples in the Upper Room. The command to love is expressed in service within a community that celebrates its unity in Jesus.

It may appear to some observers that there is little ethical teaching in John from which to forge a Christian ethic. In some ways the scarcity of commands forces a look away from the usual sources of morality (law, the world) and concentrates fully upon the person of Jesus. Such a focus undoubtedly results in calling upon God for the wherewithal to love as Jesus loved. There is little specifically ethical teaching in the fourth gospel because the reader is called to a total commitment to Jesus himself, and not to his teachings.

Early Christianity is often pictured as a universal and open movement, including all kinds of people. Yet in John's gospel there seems to be a narrowness in the exclusive commandment to Christians to love only one another. According to some biblical scholars, John represented or was concerned for a community of Christians who were seriously threatened by dangerous misconceptions about the faith. For instance, a popular idea among many early Christians was that Jesus as the holy Son of God could not possibly have defiled himself to "become flesh" and live as a fully human being in the world. The ethical conclusions of these Christians (the "Gnostics") tended to encourage irresponsibility toward the world—no service, no togetherness in the church. It is clear that the ethic of John is not an ethic for popular consumption because the love called for has a dark side that is rejected by many. God's son Jesus was put to death. But the early church needed to deal with these questions. How are the faithful to believe? Is the risen Christ the same as the earthly Jesus? Perhaps understandably, the erosion of these ideas of faith came as much from within the church as from without.

There is in John, therefore, something that was critically important to the early church. This is the affirmation of the uncompromising love of God for this world, a love that expressed itself in Christ in the most vulnerable manner possible. Thus the tough nature of love must be seen and recognized for what it is on the one hand, while the self-giving and unforced nature of love must also be observed on the other. This does not mean a hatred of the world. Indeed, hatred is never called for by John.

This love ethic is "moral" and "Christian" in the profound sense of mandating a way of life and warning about avoiding compromises as the church made its way into the world. It sets out the Christian imitation of God in the clearest and most dramatic terms. The love of God in Christ was not compromised, although it was vulnerable to humanity's abuse since it had to be open to acceptance. The love of human beings for human beings shares this same total commitment that at the same time opens it to rejection. But it is not open to compromise. Such love resists eclecticism. Its conciliation is a one-sided affair, bringing people from the world into Christ.

It must be made clear that for John the only way in which the world will know of God in Christ is through the loving unity and mutual service present in the church (among disciples). This places a great burden on the ethical life of the church. It is a radical ethic, boldly stated in absolutes, with a heavy burden attached to it. But it must never be forgotten that it is an ethic for which the disciples are promised help. They may ask what is necessary knowing that and divine power and wisdom are with them through the Holy Spirit.

Johannine Ethics Today

Many might reject John as a source for contemporary Christian ethics because of his exclusive, world-rejecting narrowness. It is people, not God, who polarize by their rejection of God's love. The gospel clearly spoke to the church of the first century. But that fact cannot necessarily lead Christians today to assume that John's ethics were warmly appreciated or deeply understood, even then. If they were discerned and appreciated, John provided a balance or counterweight to the prevailing tendency of the church to seek a good arrangement, even compromise, with Rome and the world. In the proliferation of ethical materials developing in the church, the Johannine focus demonstrated the need to maintain a uniquely Christian emphasis.

The apparent failure of John's ethic to be "doable" is a problem. Such failure, however, results from not being faithful in Christ. Today's negative criticism of John is based not so much on his inadequacies as an ethical teacher, but on a modern stance with regard to studying biblical ethics. Too often Christians have assumed that ethics will need to be accommodated to the world in some way. A Christian ethic should center on love in an emotional, warm, personal, and private manner. And it should focus outwardly on questions of peace and social justice. John's view does none of these things. The task of John's readers today is not to judge his ethic by contemporary standards, but to understand his position, the situation from which it came, and those to whom it was directed.

John calls the faithful today to a life of uncompromising love, somehow organized to issue concretely in service. This simplicity of focus—concrete and helpful love—does not mean that the Christian life is simple-minded, nor does it suggest a withdrawn or anti-possessions lifestyle. Instead John gives a strong and singular call to the one unifying and fundamental feature of the Christian ethic: love.

Questions for Reflection

1. What would it mean for us to love everyone? Consider the pros and cons of loving everyone versus the idea of Christians only loving other Christians.

2. Who teaches us today—the Jesus of first century Palestine or the living Christ, now risen to be with God? What difference might there be between the two teachers?

3. Do you have difficulties with the "simplicity" of this chapter's analysis of John? What do you think the "simple life" is? What is it that makes life "simple"?

4. Is it possible to express the incarnation type of love found in Jesus without some sort of structure and unity? If so, how? If not, what forms of unity have you found that best express such love?

Suggestions for Further Reading

Raymond Brown, *The Community of the Beloved Disciple*, New York: Paulist Press, 1979. Discusses the nature of the church as addressed by John.

Clinton D. Morrison, "Mission and Ethic: An Interpretation of John 17," *Interpretation* 19 (1965): 259-273. Makes a case for the nature of the church's mission as an effort to resist compromising the gospel in any way, shape, or form.

Pheme Perkins, *Love Commands in the New Testament,* New York: Paulist Press, 1982. examines several love commands in a form helpful for Bible study or Sunday School class.

D. Bruce Whol, *Johannine Christianity in Conflict*, SBL Dissertation Series #60, Chico, Calif.: Scholars Press, 1981. An examination of how the authority of the historical Jesus and that of the risen Christ are related.

Conclusion
Toward a New Testament Ethic

In the New Testament, God used many voices and many pictures to show the Christian life. This is an exciting thought. It offers encouragement and challenge as Christians today seek to deepen their participation in the life of discipleship. In this study we have found that each New Testament writer explores the Christian moral life in ways that are uniquely adapted to his own setting in life, and that his ethical views flow genuinely from his own experience with Christ as savior.

The New Testament is a rich chorus of such experiences. Christians today are members of the same community of faith, and are invited to dialogue with those early witnesses. They are encouraged to develop their own ethical responses that are faithful to that which God has accomplished in Christ Jesus. Believers are challenged to assume this opportunity in dialogue with those New Testament writers.

The purpose of the preceding chapters has been to encourage us to hear the unique ethical conceptions and contributions of eight New Testament writers. We have found that each writer does indeed have a distinctive moral "personality" or point of view, an individual version of what the Christian life is. We saw how each writer dealt with particular problems that confronted and interested him and the audience for whom the book or letter was written. The scripture passages selected for comment certainly do not exhaust the possibilities for edification and study. Much conversation lies ahead; much more can be learned. While there has been limited discussion of specific ethical commands, the heart of our discovery has been that each writer testifies to a unique experience with Christ. That experience is then translated into a Christian lifestyle.

While we have not dwelt on the reasons for the behavior advocated in each book or letter, we have seen that Christian *doing* grows out of Christian *being*. The uniqueness of New Testament ethics is found in the orientation provided by the new life in Christ. His was a life focused on others which provides not only motivation but power for a new life in a new community.

In light of the vast array of differences among the writers, is there any way to find a central or common denominator? Is there a summary of New Testament ethics, other than the fact that all of these voices are found in the New Testament and that all are centered in the Christian experience? What, if any, is the controlling thread that runs through lives of discipleship, regardless of the century and location where they are lived?

There do seem to be certain generalities that are both accurate and useful with regard to a "New Testament ethic." Yet we need to be cautious about introducing them at this point. There is no suggestion here that the New Testament chorus of ethical voices can be reduced to a single voice. The following characteristics are found throughout the variety of writings studied: The ethical viewpoints developed were Christ-centered in origin and motivation, social in their impact, and presented with the conviction that God continues to provide the necessary support for Christians to live the life of discipleship. Let's elaborate.

First, there is a richness in the variety of responses to the gift of salvation through Christ. Each writer receives it, processes it, and applies it in slightly different ways. It is clear in the New Testament documents that there are problems facing the early church that were in the process of being resolved. Some of these problems overlap from writer to writer, and each of them relies on the presence of the living Lord to work them out. One of these issues is that of the relationship of Christians to the world; another is that of the nature or definition of Christian community. The light that these unique perspectives cast on the mission and witness of the contemporary church is important. They create a dialogue that can broaden the current points of view and help us see things we did not see before. For example, Peter's notion of suffering as a measure of the Christian life is certainly foreign to many Christians today and different from the theme of adjustment to the world presented by Mark. The "dialogue" found within the New Testament thus becomes a discussion into which the church today can enter. In doing so, we can expect to be helped in our own situations by the early Christians.

Variety, however, does not mean that "anything goes." It does not mean that anyone can propose any ethic and claim that it is authentically Christian. It does mean—and this is a second conclusion—that each ethic is derived from, centered in, and motivated by Christ. The relationship that the Christian has with Christ is that of a new person, a servant, and one who will be judged. Each moral point of view is the result of a Christian thoughtfully working out in everyday life the transformation wrought by God in Christ. The ethic is varied because Christ is not simply a teacher who passes out a moral codes, or sets up a new system of values. It is varied because Christ has transformed the Christian into a new, but still unique, person.

A third generalization that has emerged has to do with the social nature of ethics. Since Christ has brought Christians to himself, they need not be devoted to themselves. Christ has made changes in people that make life different. Although this begins with the individual's personal transformation and commitment, there is also a great deal of concern for others as the specific objects of God's love in Christ.

God's will is only realized when individual people are fully integrated into a new and divinely provided life. It is important, therefore, to keep in mind "what is going on here." There is a new community and a new set of relationships in which some things have clearly happened. People have been brought together in spite of nationality, religiosity, condition of health, social status, or political

persuasion. The ethical views we have studied are all efforts
to explore and structure this new community and its
relationship to the world. Indeed, it could be said that the
universal goal of Christian ethics is to enhance the lives of all
who share in the community (with the hope of some positive
spill-over to others outside).

The communal dimension is important to understand
because individual decisions are made within the faith community. The early church contained greater social diversity
than any other institution within the Roman Empire. The
relationship of the local Christian groups to the secular
world tended to vary from place to place and from time to
time. The church today still has these same problems
because it has remained a universal institution, incorporat-
ing persons of all national background, cultures, and com-
mitments. As within the New Testament, this variety can be
seen as an opportunity to fashion the Christian life in
many ways.

In the fourth place, we are free moral agents, not controlled by outside forces. Some Christians feel that people
are under the influence of evil forces that interfere with
one's ability to live on the ethical level desired. In the New
Testament the devil occasionally suggests courses of action
against divine will (as in the "wilderness experience" of
Jesus). The preponderant view of the New Testament
writers, however, is that the devil is not in control of human
behavior. The real problem is the mystery of sin. Why is it
that humans so often prefer to choose the evil? Even under
the severest of conditions, as in 1 Peter, Christians are counseled not to give in. Never is "the devil made me do it" an acceptable excuse for not living the Christian life. In the New
Testament the devil only has the power to tempt, not to
command.

Each of the New Testament writers studied in this survey unquestionably believes that the ethical commandments
they describe can be performed or achieved. This is because
God is with them through the presence and power of the
Holy Spirit. As is clear from John, and may be assumed from
what others wrote, they trusted in God for the reality of their

transformed live. They now could and must live new lives in accordance with Christ's will.

These are some features common to all New Testament writers as they formulated ethical responses to problems they faced. Are there not some *specific* ethical commands to be found in *all* the writers? The most frequent expectation is that of love. But even with this apparently universal goal, there are individual differences. For instance, if we ask, "Whom are we to love?," various writers provide slightly different answers. James would have Christians love all people equally. Hebrews and Luke would have Christ's followers love outsiders especially. And then there is John, who would have the faithful concentrate almost exclusively on loving other Christians. Can these points of disagreement be resolved or harmonized? What is *the* Christian or truly New Testament ethic on love?

But why should there be just one definition, or one ethic? Why cannot we allow the unique individuals whom God loved and chose in the first century to speak and let their words stand without forcing them into categories that satisfy some personal need we might have for neatness and uniformity? As God sent Christ to become "flesh" in Jesus (John 1:14), so has God seen fit to use a variety of individual voices and experiences in producing the New Testament. Modern readers need to take seriously the New Testament writers as real people and the unique expressions of the Christian life that they reveal. The variety within the New Testament ethical witness resists any kind of final summary or reduction. The dialogue within the New Testament cannot be reduced to a monologue. Their voices should not be forced to agree with our own. Instead, today's readers may be drawn into that ongoing and exciting dialogue.

Are Christian ethics unique? Clearly there is an emphasis on love and related characteristics of ethical living. These are certainly not confined solely to Christianity. New Testament ethics are unique because of the reasons the New Testament writer gave for their importance and the motivation or resources that made them desirable and possible.

How do these ethical views apply to contemporary faith and the mission and witness of the church? It must be said initially that these ethics are useful only to those who share the basic faith confession of the New Testament writers: in Christ is true life and from him flows the appropriate moral life. Christ calls individuals, transforms them, creates them into new communities.

The first consideration in applying New Testament ethics to our personal situation is to let them truly speak. If they apply to a topic or address a train of thought we do not care to hear—let them speak. Christians must not overlay their own concerns and answers on the words of scripture. As the New Testament writers speak, listen for how those Christians related their belief in Christ to the way they lived in everyday life and in crisis situations. Let those voices question and challenge. Let them pose ethical questions for present day situations. Let them ask us about a contemporary vision of the Christian life, attitudes toward the world, the nature of the reborn Christian personality, and current ethical issues. The experience of New Testament writers struggling with ethical decisions is a precedent for Christians today. They challenge us individually and corporately to be faithful in living out new life in Christ.

This "conversation" with New Testament writers is an ongoing one. If we go to the scriptures only when we have a problem to solve, it is difficult to have a long-term opportunity to form and develop Christian "character." Serious and disciplined study of scripture exposes the reader to patterns of faith that help forge a Christian personality. The experiences of the New Testament writers provide patterns of faith against which to measure the practical applications of our beliefs. We cannot be content with occasionally resorting to scripture for assistance; that is a frivolous misuse of the Bible. Such an approach ignores the uniqueness of the biblical writers and relies on our own ideas in selecting, arranging, and applying the texts as *we* see fit—"proof texting" as it is sometimes called. This approach, although popular with many, is really not a serious one to the Bible.

It is far better to study and dialogue with the Bible in a systematic, ongoing, and disciplined manner. In this way, the

Christian's mind is formed by what is read and understanding increases. Then, when a particular ethical question does arise, it will be possible to respond in a way that is natural, in a way that flows both from individual beliefs and from the witness of the scriptures. We need to be centered in a community of conversation with New Testament writers, allowing their ideas to permeate our faith commitment, letting their assessment of life situations (many of which will be similar to those we face) challenge and stimulate us. Out of that involvement and engagement we can be ready to bring our own faith in Christ to bear on moral decisions. The basic fidelities are always to Christ and those for whom he died. This introduction to New Testament ethics has shown how some of our earliest Christian brothers have faced that faith challenge.

The immediate task in this study—that of tuning in as clearly as possible to eight New Testament voices on the subject of the Christian discipleship—is now complete. But the opportunities are just beginning. There are many more biblical writers to be heard from and a lifetime of opportunities in which to hear and see, responding to others out of Christian faith. This is what Paul meant when he wrote: "work out your own salvation in fear and trembling (Phil. 2:12)." He did not mean that salvation was to be created by his readers, but that it had been given by God and now it was up to the readers to live it out, express it, make it real in the world.

New Testament ethical statements and implications are not the last word in developing Christian ethics. There are difficulties yet unsolved. There are disagreements. There are problems today that were unimagined in the first century. Instead of seeing in the New Testament the *last word,* perhaps it would be better to see it as the *first* word. Instead of using the Bible as a textbook to which we run for answers, let us engage in serious conversation with its authors. Instead of simply hearing New Testament commandments as a code to live by, let us be invigorated by its words of faith, challenge, encouragement, and call to commitment. Instead of using scripture as a last resort for solving problems, let us allow it to form the character of those new beings that we become in Christ Jesus.

Appendix One
Jesus the Teacher

It is a common assumption that Jesus was primarily, or most importantly, a teacher of morality, both in his words and in his deeds. Any book about the ethical teaching of the New Testament could be expected to agree with this popular perception. Indeed, many people cling to this perception of Jesus' character and importance even though they do not adhere to other tenets of the Christian faith such as Jesus' divinity, and the centrality of his death and resurrection as the basis for salvation by faith.

It should be noted, however, that a number of the writers considered in this book impress an ethical outlook upon the reader without naming Jesus as teacher and without referring explicitly to his teachings. The writers of Hebrews, the letters of Paul, and 1 Peter are examples. For these writers, the most important thing about Jesus was his death and triumphant resurrection. Their views of the Christian life, morality, and discipleship were founded upon and developed within the framework of the central work of Christ as Son of God, Son of Man, Redeemer, Lord—in short, within a much richer understanding of who Jesus was and what God accomplished through him.

With Matthew, Mark, Luke, and John, however, it might appear to be a different story—one which is probably more familiar to most Christians. These writers present a Jesus who instructs his disciples—a Jesus whose life story (not just death story) is told. The gospel presentation of Jesus as teacher merits a closer look.

In Mark, the second most frequently used title for Jesus is that of "teacher" (twelve times). Some of his teaching is about himself (8:31; 9:31). He also gives a large number of commands such as: "Come here!" (3:3); "Sit down!" (6:39). Obviously these cannot be taken as ethical commands. There are others, however, which may appear to be ethical commands: "Follow me!" (1:17) or "Feed them!" (6:37). Mark tells us *where* Jesus taught: in the synagogue (6:2); in the villages (6:6). He describes *how* he taught: in parables. He reports the response to his teaching: astonishment (1:22; 11:18). The fact that teaching was typical and routine for Jesus is absolutely clear (6:6,34; 14:49). But what surprises us is that Mark shows so little interest in the content and details of *what* Jesus taught. Since there is so little teaching material that is explicitly ethical, Mark's ethical outlook may be sought in the miracle passages. Surely these stories indicate the kind of world Jesus wanted. Jesus was more than a teacher who merely exhorted others or described the future. He made wholeness for others a reality. Jesus was called "teacher" when he performed miracles: calming the storm (4:38); raising the dead (5:35); healing the epileptic (9:17). He is a teacher, but he cannot be simply a teacher; he is much more.

In Matthew, Jesus is called "teacher" nine times. In every case but one the person or persons addressing him are neither disciples nor followers; in fact, they are often antagonists. The exception is 26:18 where Jesus refers to himself as "teacher." This has led one scholar to pose a distinction between the title of teacher and that of Lord, suggesting that only strangers and antagonists refer to Jesus as "teacher," while the disciples call him Lord. Another scholar believes that the designation of Jesus as teacher by the religious leaders of that day was a form of criticism. The title implied that Jesus was *only* a teacher, and a false one at that.

Matthew shows his opposition to this view of Jesus by placing the Sermon on the Mount in a prominent role—at the beginning of the gospel. He is a teacher even greater than Moses, but it is his death and resurrection that put his teaching in its proper perspective. As with Mark, the reader must seek beyond the simple category of teacher for a full indication of the kind of ethical outlook that is central to Matthew. Again, Jesus is a teacher, but to avoid misunderstanding his role, those who follow him must not call him teacher. Rather, he is a teacher who fulfills what he commands. He is a teacher who continues his presence and teaching in the community after his death (Matt. 28:20).

In Luke, Jesus is called teacher thirteen times, more often by antagonists (Pharisees, Sadducees, scribes) than by disciples (7:40) or supplicants hoping for miracles (8:49 and 9:38). As in Mark, only once does Jesus refer to himself as a teacher (22:11). Even in a gospel with a great deal of teaching material (the special long travel narrative), the frequency of the designation teacher runs a poor second to that of Lord. According to John's gospel it is the Holy Spirit who will teach and remind us of the words of Jesus. It is only in the light of the triumphant and resurrected Jesus that his words have significance for our lives. He cannot be extracted from the gospel and turned into a mere ethics instructor. As Mary tried to grasp "my teacher" in the garden (John 20:16–17), Jesus continues to resist our efforts to reduce him to and possess him as our teacher.

In Paul's letters, 1 Peter, and Hebrews, the term "teacher" is not used, although the teachings of Jesus frequently can be detected beneath the words of each writer. This clearly shows that the early church never believed Jesus was simply a teacher whose words merely needed to be communicated. Rather he was always the Lord, whose words remain significant because he died and rose for us.

It is only James who seems to have remembered Jesus as primarily a teacher. For James, the picture of Jesus is that of one who commanded believers to fulfill the law; he then left with the promise/threat to return someday to judge how the disciples had fared in his absence. There is no reference in James to grace, mercy, or forgiveness; there is no reference to the sacrificial death of Jesus and the triumphant resurrection.

But if James *is* right, and Jesus is only a teacher, we are most miserable—because those teachings are so demanding and we are left hopelessly inadequate. It seems better to see

Jesus' teaching as a part of the whole of his saving work. By this work we have been redeemed into a new reality which each writer describes uniquely. The specific teachings are some of the details in a larger picture that must be worked at in the daily lives of Christians for whom Jesus Christ continues to act as Lord. These New Testament documents are the first word, not the last, on ethics.

Appendix Two
Rewards and Punishments

If salvation is by grace, the idea of reward and punishment seems contradictory and irrelevant. If Christ came to reveal the love of God, then the notion of reward and punishment undermines his gracious efforts on our behalf. If the Christian life is rooted in what Christ has done for us, and if each New Testament writer has shown his understanding of Christ's work, then a simple reward and punishment ethic would be an insult to the purpose of each New Testament writer and to the intent of God in Christ.

Very often, however, people think moral behavior and ethics are prompted by the threat of punishment or the promise of reward. This is a common and popular assumption, but one that has little basis in fact. A careful reading of the New Testament reveals that hope for reward and fear of punishment are *not* the primary reasons New Testament writers give for living the life of discipleship.

Each chapter of this book has described the basis on which the New Testament authors urge the adoption of a certain ethical outlook or behavior. In *no* case was reward or punishment a primary factor. What does it mean, then, when a writer used the language of reward and punishment? A survey of pertinent material is necessarily brief (precisely because there is so little of it) and will serve to place the occasional reward and punishment language in its proper perspective. A quick summary of the terms "punish" and "reward" and related words (punished, rewarded) reveals the following:

Term: occurs in	Matt.	Mark	Luke	John	Peter	Paul	Heb.	James	Total
Reward	12	1	3	0	0	4	2	0	22
Wages	1	0	2	1	0	3	0	1	8
Punish	2	0	1	0	1	5	2	0	11
Total	15	1	6	1	1	12	4	1	41

In Peter, Mark, John, and James, there is only one occurrence of these terms. Because language is indicative of thought, it seems reasonable to assume that the writers who do not use the language of reward and punishment avoided it for a reason. The single exception is James—the only writer who takes a reward and punishment view of the Christian life. James says that each person is responsible for obeying the whole law and each will be judged according to that law. This idea is not found in Mark, John, or 1 Peter. It would be very difficult to construct a reward and punishment ethic from Mark, John, or 1 Peter unless one were to read it *into* the text.

Most occurrences of these terms are found in Matthew. There, the judgment of God takes a dynamic role in creating the context within which ethics are formed. Matthew's understanding of this judgment (chapter 25) presents information about the standards God will use. The reader discovers in this passage what is God's will. Matthew's clear intention is to encourage his readers to live creatively according to that will. If there were to be a judgment according to the absolute will of God, Matthew would have had no practical or pastoral reason for writing the gospel story. If judgement were only a threat, there would be no way to know *what* believers are exhorted to do.

The idea of reward for services rendered *is* an important theme in Luke. Several Lucan passages speak of reward. There are heavenly rewards (6:23b; 14:14), sometimes tied directly to the right use of money (16:9). There are also earthly rewards, some of which are to be avoided (14:12b), but some of which are also appropriate for disciples. The promise of earthly reward is controlled by the Lucan idea of servanthood. The appropriate earthly rewards have to do with the necessary sustenance of the disciple and they are contrasted with the self-serving rewards sought by the worldly—those whose lives are calculated in terms of investment and payoff.

The idea of reward need not conjure up negative thoughts of a "works righteousness." Instead, it is rooted in the idea of the trustworthiness of God as a just master. Luke tells several master and servant parables that describe a master who is reliable, and supportive—not quixotic. Luke believes that God will care for his people. Far from representing a business transaction, Luke's gospel points toward a relationship in which each party cares for the other's needs while allowing the other to reciprocate in the most appropriate manner. Reward is simply an expected part of God's faithfulness.

Luke's frequent mention of reward seems to indicate a healthy interest in the ongoing life of the church in the world. "Reward" might be construed as moving closer to the master—as in the Parable of the Talents. By contrast the ethic developed in Hebrews is fundamentally grounded in the vision of who Christ is, and what he has done to transform the lives of his followers. His work as priest and sacrifice has changed the faith community from sacrificers with bad consciences (because of the continual inadequacy of the sacrifices offered) into servants of God who can now offer the sacrifices of love and good works to friends and strangers alike. However, there are a number of passages in Hebrews that in isolation might imply some notion of reward and punishment. Though Christ is not the judge even in his second coming (9:27–28b), Hebrews still includes the Jewish idea of a coming (day of) judgment (1:12; 2:2; 4:1; 6:8; 9:27; 10:25, 27; 12:23, 27–29; 13:4b). What is the nature of that judgment and how does it relate to the ethical activity of Christians?

The writer of Hebrews warns that it is difficult if not impossible for Christians who have turned away from their faith to repent and be restored once again (10:26b; 12:17). If one turns back, one falls into sin. Sin is a "different place"; it is not like living with the vision of Christ the High Priest and sacrifice. Sacrifice cannot make up for sin; thus the sinner is lost and judgment is the inevitable fate. But Christians will not suffer judgment since they are already freed from sin and its accompanying uneasy conscience. Judgment is simply not a part of the new experience that the Christian has received as a result of Christ's work. The threat of judgment should not be read as a warning but as a negative reminder of who the readers now are, and in what condition they now live.

Promises of reward in Hebrews ought to be read in the same light. They too are descriptive of the new situation; they are not carrots held up to encourage people to follow certain ethical paths. The real encouragement for the new lifestyle is found in Christ's work. It is work which transforms the lives of persons who approach God. Christians are no longer bound by ritualistic sacrifice, but rather they are encouraged and enabled to support all people in a loving community.

The commands found in chapter thirteen support this idea. In this section the author concentrates his ethical instruction (1-5, 7, 9, 13, 16-17, 19); however, reasons are added in only a few (4-5, 16, 17, 19). It is difficult in some cases to see why the particular threat or reward is attached. There are comments attached to virtually all of the ethical exhortations. In most cases they are neither rewards nor threats, but comments on the nature of the activity or the nature of the Christian life (vv. 2-3, 9, 13). Christian life is viewed as a whole; suggestions of benefits and warnings of judgement serve as reminders of the character of this new life. There is no way that the ethics of Hebrews could be reduced to a list of behaviors and their accompanying rewards or punishments.

In light of this study, those rare verses (2 Thes. 1:9; Heb. 10:29) that promise a heavenly reward for earthly faithfulness and good behavior cannot possibly be the most important guiding ethic for living the Christian life. These passages are too few to represent the predominant early Christian view. They contradict both the general thrust of an ethic based on a new life experience and the explicit denials that such a basis is proper. In fact, a number of specific rejections of the reward and punishment orientation can be found in Romans 4:4 and 6:23. Living the Christian life simply to earn a reward is inconsistent with the New Testament message. The occasional mention of reward and punishment expresses the importance of the Christian ethical life and the urgency of applying oneself seriously to it. Often the idea of reward and punishment is incorporated in poetic imagery which describes the relationship of mankind to God. Very often the Christian reader simply assumes that one is blindly obligated by God to live the Christian life—that life will be more rewarding if it is lived a certain way. Some are afraid not to live the Christian life. These childish notions must be left behind. They are simply not supported by the moral visions of the New Testament writers.